The Anaïs Nin Literary Journal

Edited by Paul Herron   Volume 1, 2003

Editor's Note

When Richard Centing and Benjamin Franklin V issued *Under the Sign of Pisces*, the first Nin-based periodical, Anaïs Nin responded:

> *I call it "the Café in Space." I hope it makes a link between all of us who have common interests.*
>
> *It is so difficult to sustain links between us because of great geographical distances. We do not have time to write long letters. But many friendships have formed around my work, many connections* (Diary 7 *127-128*).

With this inaugural issue of *A Café in Space: The Anaïs Nin Literary Journal*, we hope to continue the idea of making "a link between all of us," to continue the good work begun by *Under the Sign of Pisces* and furthered by the superb *ANAIS: An International Journal*.

This year we celebrate Anaïs Nin's birth one hundred years ago. The centennial gives us all an opportunity to reflect on the life Anaïs Nin created for herself and the extraordinary document that goes along with it, her *Diary*.

It was Gunther Stuhlmann's plan to release a special centennial issue of *ANAIS: An International Journal* this year, but illness did not allow him to see it through. *A Café in Space* is thus inspired by and is meant to be a tribute to both Anaïs Nin and Gunther Stuhlmann. Some of the articles in this issue were originally intended for *ANAIS*, and we are happy to be able to include them here for our readers.

During the past few years, the Nin community has lost some very important members. Gunther, the standard-bearer of Anaïs Nin's work for nearly fifty years, passed away April 1, 2002. His leadership, vast knowledge, and wisdom will be missed sorely, beyond what simple words can convey. Sharon Spencer died exactly one week later. Not only did Sharon share friendship with Anaïs, she also devoted much of her academic career promoting her work, especially with her book *Collage of Dreams*. Daisy Aldan, with whom Anaïs Nin shared the trials of being a woman artist self-publishing in America, passed away in February of 2001. Daisy's artistic genius and inspirational spirit made her a very special and much loved person, and her work as both poet and translator is legendary. Evelyn Hinz, whose *Mirror and the Garden* is considered by many to be one of the most insightful books written on Nin's work, died in December 2002, after a long and distinguished career at the University of Manitoba. While we celebrate the centennial, may we also remember the lives and contributions of these brilliant individuals.

The circle still widens, however, and a "new breed" of Nin readers and scholars is emerging. They remind us that there is really only one way to understand and appreciate Anaïs Nin, and that is to read her work. Within the pages of this journal, we shall be able to share what we learn from it.

A Café in Space is an annual publication, due out each summer, and we welcome submissions of articles or proposals having to do with Anaïs Nin and her circle.

Our associated web site, which can be found by going to www.skybluepress.com, is designed to enhance the information found in the journal. Each article, whenever appropriate, will have links associated with the topic, more detailed material or photographs, and ways to give feedback, ask questions, help facilitate research. It is our sincere hope that with the journal and web site, we will be able to form a "café" in which Nin scholars, readers, and those with parallel interests will gather. Nin study is hampered by a lack of communication between those of us who engage in it, and this is a way to address the problem. We encourage you to "spread the word" so that we can build a strong central base of Nin scholarship and readership.

In this issue, we have included a special selection of work from Japan. The contributions of Kazuko Sugisaki, Yuko Yaguchi, and Toyoko Yamamoto represent the degree to which Japanese interest in Anaïs Nin has risen. There has been a surge of activity in Japan, the latest being Kazuko Sugisaki's translation of *Incest*. There are several books dealing with Nin that have recently been published, and some of them are examined here.

On April 12, 2003, a conference entitled "Anaïs Nin: A Writer, A Life" was held in Santa Barbara, California. The contributions by Janet Fitch and Aeryn Seto are taken from the transcripts of their talks. Other speakers included Kazuko Sugisaki, whose article is based on her talk, Tristine Rainer, Karin Finell, and Paul Herron.

Daisy Aldan's "Flight" is taken from her last poetry book, *Collected Poems of Daisy Aldan*, Sky Blue Press, 2002.

Shymal Bagchee's "thinking homes" is from his forthcoming poetry collection, *Gabardine and Other Poems*.

Dudley Levenson's "Appreciating Gunther Stuhlmann" originally appeared in *The Artful Mind*.

Acknowledgements

The Editor would like to thank the following for their assistance in the realization of this issue:

Rupert Pole and the Anaïs Nin Trust for permissions to use quotations from Anaïs Nin's work, and for photographic material.
Barbara Stuhlmann for her encouragement and guidance.
Sara Herron, without whom none of this would be possible.
Jacques and Monique Laÿ and Anne-Marie Thomas for organizing the visit in Louveciennes.
Jean-Hugues Anglade for the tour of 2 bis rue de Montbuisson.
Joaquín Nin-Culmell for his hospitality and insight.
Denise Brown for her support.
The University Press of Florida, Edgework Books, and Northern Illinois University Press for providing review copies.
Roger Jackson for sowing ideas and for his continual support.
Claudine Brelet, Thomas March, Suzanne Zuccaro, Karin Finell, Karl Orend.

A Café in Space: the Anaïs Nin Literary Journal is published annually by Sky Blue Press, 3438 Kilmer, Troy, MI 48083 USA, and edited by Paul Herron.

Submissions or proposals should be directed to the above address. Material may also be submitted by attaching a Word document to an e-mail message sent to skybluepress@skybluepress.com. Please identify the contents in the subject line or it will not be opened.

Any unsolicited material will not be returned without inclusion of a self-addressed and stamped envelope. Safety of manuscripts and other materials is not the responsibility of Sky Blue Press.

ISBN: 0-9652364-8-X

Sky Blue Press
Troy, MI

True to Character
A letter to girls who write diaries

ike you, I was fourteen years old.
The lesbian in second period said:
"Henry and June. You've never read it?"
On the cover a man, a woman, a Parisian bridge, dawn,
He knelt before her. Her leg slung over his shoulder.
Be ready to quit every country
To exhaust every thing you come to possess
Except this:

She writes, *"I am in bliss. This is the life, the talk, these are the emotions
which belong to me. I breathe freely now. I am at home. I am myself"* (88).

It was everything I wanted out of life,
You are free to make it yours
"Unexpurgated?" I breathed.
"You can borrow it."
I saw the stories I would make my own.

She writes, *"I want to bite into life, and to be torn by it"* (179).

I used to leave notebooks barely touched. Her diary
Gave me mouth and hands to narrate
And what I created was passion.
There was to be no word about the mundane: skinniness, braces,
No, you too will write maps of your desire for love, your desire for life.
Put down every voluptuous thing you believe before your senses
are corrupted by experience.
As a virgin you know everything.
I believed I knew what to do with a man: Anaïs taught me
in Henry's bedroom at Clichy. I knew how to make a man love me,
seeing how she stole their imaginations,
falling in love with the woman they saw,
Learned how to enslave him as I saw her coy before her analyst
and suddenly fussy before her husband; how to resist him
as I saw her inch away from her cousin Eduardo
in a café in Montparnasse, fixing him from under downcast lashes.
You'll use all this. To travel, to love;

above all, to have something to write about.

She writes, "*To make life more interesting. To imitate literature, which is a hoax*" (206).

Two things happen when you fall in love.
You will become yourself. And your diary will get good.
Of course it was bound to happen this way,
the way I had seen in it in another woman's journal.
Later you must do another thing you've read about: leave.

She writes, "*What he does not know is that I must complete the unfulfilled portions of my life, that I must have what I have missed so far, to complete myself and my own story*" (159).

Your heroine will find a better setting elsewhere.
Here's your curse, and if he comes to find you,
he'll weep saying you're no longer his, that he can feel it.
Believe in love. You'll forget
how love is born: as your self is born, as a story is born.
Just like in the diary.
They will only wish to be near you as they know you,
you at your best, you being loved by them. You as you must exist in
    your story.
Do you think you can be naked? Be ready
To have your heart broken first.

She writes, "*I affect their imaginations. It is the strongest power*" (54).

If love is what you want, be ready to quit every country
You'll exhaust every thing you come to possess
Perhaps someday you, too, will lie down the journal and want to die
Summon your last strength to make a new story.

She writes, "*...Nothing too long imagined can be perfect in a worldly way*" (24).

It's against your instinct, I know,
But this is inevitable:
You will betray people
As long as you are true to the character you've created,
To the woman you wrote out in these pages.

She writes, "*I would deceive the greatest and finest man on earth*" (229).

Don't answer a man who asks
how many men you've loved. Only say: "I've never betrayed."
Let every terrible kiss vanish
Out of allegiance to the story you are telling.

She writes, "*The journal is a product of my disease, perhaps an accentuation
and exaggeration of it. I speak of relief when I write; perhaps, but it is also an
engraving of pain, a tattooing of myself*" (207).

Fill notebooks, roam
love to love and country to country,
packing the lines with stories.
Though you will be accused by men
more than once of being inconsistent, of being faithless,
you must never doubt your loyalty to one thing:
that journal, and what it means to you
will be the love of the character you are becoming.

She writes, "*Last night I wept. I wept because the process by which I have
become a woman was painful. I wept because I was no longer a child with a
child's blind faith… I wept because I could not believe anymore and I love to
believe. I can still love passionately without believing… I wept because I have
lost my pain and am not yet accustomed to its absence*" (274).

Maybe you're wondering about your fate: you'll find
your destruction where your sustenance came from.
I adjure you: when joy was taken from me
I, gripping paper and pen to set it all down
I had no hands to fight with.

She writes, "*My instincts lead me to love over and over again*" (238).

Over and over you'll build and abandon
The love you are looking for.
It won't wave with the strung banners
Of laundry in the alleys of Naples,
Take the stairs from Montmartre.
It won't stretch nude, after all, on an Andalucian bed
While the cicadas hum in the heat
It knows nothing of Amsterdam and rain.
It will already have been there

Cramping inside you, regardless of the scenery. It didn't need to be written
On that train, flying past some high village
Or singing songs with strangers on the platform.
The seed was there to begin with.
You wrote the map before you set off.
When you come to the bridge at the riverbank
You'll find yourself alone. I suggest
You bring a notebook. ❖

All quotations taken from: Nin, Anaïs. Henry and June: From A Journal of Love. The Unexpurgated Diary of Anaïs Nin 1931-1932. *New York: Harcourt Brace and Company, 1989.*

Anaïs Nin in California, 1970s
Photo © Anaïs Nin Trust

Janet Fitch

No Women Writers
My introduction to Anaïs Nin

q would like to discuss the effect Anaïs Nin had on me personally, and on a generation of women writers and artists, how she affected and inspired us.

I met Anaïs Nin in 1969. Not in the flesh, but on the page, the way most of us encountered her. I was in junior high, fourteen years old. One day, our English teacher was out, and we got a substitute teacher instead, a man who maintained that there were no important women writers. He challenged our class to think of a single one.

I can still remember the frustration I felt that day—I knew there had to be some, but it was a tribute to the educational system I grew up in that I could not think of a single one. At the time, I had not heard of Virginia Woolf, nor Edith Wharton, not Colette or George Sand, not even Willa Cather. I had read the Brontës, but they didn't occur to me at that frustrating and humiliating moment—of which there had been so many in early life, so many "women can't" or "women don't"... I just wanted to cry, because I was so inadequate, and knew so little, and was so unable to defend my sex.

And then a girl in the front row raised her hand, I can still see her, her frizzy ash-blonde hair, her plump arm, waving, and she asked, What about Anaïs Nin?

Thank god for this girl. I still remember her name, Abby Froelich. The teacher didn't know what to say, so in true adult style, he changed the subject. And I ripped off a note which I passed up the row... WHO IS ANAÏS NIN? Abby corrected the spelling and sent it back, saying, "Read the Diaries, they're incredible!"

So I had my mom take me out to the bookstore, and buy me the *Diaries of Anaïs Nin*. They came as a boxed set of four, 1931 to 1947. And on the box, there was this extraordinary face. Not young, not old, made up almost like a mime, very theatrical and otherworldly, but sophisticated too, the face of someone I had never met before, a woman who seemed both dreamy and hugely compassionate, as if she had heard what had gone on in the classroom that day.

So in 1969, I met Anaïs Nin for the first time.

I remember the very first entry of the diary...she was talking about her house outside of Paris, in a town called Louveciennes. It was very old and run down and very, very romantic. She described the façade of the house, which had eleven windows, and one that was just a set of closed shutters, which had been placed there for symmetry. In the diary she wrote, "I often dream about the room which does not exist beyond the closed shutter."

I was captivated by the mind that could think a thought like that. I was always being told to come down out of the clouds and be practical. The women I knew were all practical, they didn't linger in their dreams, but here was *permission* to value the secret inner life—which of course is what a room that doesn't exist, behind a closed shutter really is.

It's a very private room, that room that doesn't exist—a room in a dream, like a door you see in a dream in a house you know very well, which psychologically is your mundane everyday conscious existence. But then there's a door, and you go through the door into a room you never knew was there, this is the unknown in your own psyche.

And somehow the door was like this diary. And this fantastic figure, this Anaïs Nin, was there opening the door, suggesting that the life of the dream, the vivid life of the interior, was a beautiful, meaningful life, so naturally I embraced it as I would embrace my own secret room that didn't exist in my own growing awareness.

The next thing I encountered in the diary was her description of her house, that she had painted each room a different color, one room for each mood: "lacquer red for vehemence, pale turquoise for reveries, peach color for gentleness, green for repose, gray for work at the typewriter."

The way she had painted her house was like pulling that dream life into the outside world—which of course is also what the writer and the artist does. But at that time she was only developing as a writer, as an artist. Her house was in a way a laboratory for what she was doing inside herself. It was creating an environment to support the inner life. Now one of my favorite stories was the "Masque of the Red Death" by Edgar Allan Poe, where you go through the rooms, each a different color, to arrive at the last room, which of course (being Poe) was black with red windows. But this was a real woman, doing it for a real purpose, to support her inner life and to make it visible to herself.

Just to be that important to yourself was a revelation. The women I grew up with were all about sacrificing and repressing their needs and desires to the demands of everyday life, a life I did not want to grow up and embody. I didn't feel good about growing up to be a woman. It seemed like a life of repression of desire and personality, of self-effacement, of serving others, of being told what you can't do, because you're a woman. The books I read were about men; women only existed as the mysterious *Other*. But here was a woman who took herself as the subject of her own life, woman as subject, rather than object. Woman looking, woman thinking—about men, about love, about fear, and creation.

There was a strange disconnect in those days, when all I read about was someone other than myself. I could read Hemingway, but I couldn't be Hemingway. I read Melville, but who was I in *Moby Dick*? The inner life of his fiction had nothing to do with my own inner life. It was like being black and only reading white authors. You could appreciate the story, but there was always that depressing knowledge that the only place for you in the story was polishing shoes, or saying "yessir" in the Pullman car, a supporting player. As a woman in that male fiction, the only place for me was ironing a shirt, or cooking him dinner, or being the mysterious *Other*, the object of love.

But in Nin's diaries, I could imagine myself the subject. She was the arbiter, the narrator; it was her taste, her observations, her struggle—that was the centerpiece. Nin allowed the possibility of a direct creative life for a woman, not to be just the muse, but to be the creator.

And what a life. In the same entry, she declared, "ordinary life doesn't interest me. I seek only the high moments, I am in accord with the surrealists, searching for the marvelous."

Now as a fourteen-year-old, I knew I'd found a guide and a model. It was a time when everybody else was telling me to conform, be a good girl, get your head out of the clouds, who do you think you are? And here was someone who whispered inside my head, take a chance, don't be a good girl, stick your head in the clouds, you are someone worth knowing. You could demand the heights, if you were willing to take the chance.

So I plunged into a fascinating life—Nin's development as a writer, the creative friendships she made with other artists and writers like Henry Miller and Lawrence Durrell, Luise Rainer, Antonin Artaud, people who supported her in the life she wanted to have, giving me a clue as to how this could be done. And of course, the amazing erotic mind: she was neither good girl nor bad girl but startlingly both. And this was long before the unexpurgated diaries began to emerge, *Henry and June*, and the one about her father. It was a life worth living.

The *Diaries* led me to the fiction, a kind of writing I had never seen before: *House of Incest, Under a Glass Bell*, novellas in *Winter of Artifice*, and the beautiful interlinked novels that together are the *Cities of the Interior*, with names such as *Ladders to Fire, A Spy in the House of Love*, and *Seduction of the Minotaur*—revealing a subterranean world of the watery or fiery emotions, the internal terrain of the female psyche.

The fiction was, in certain ways even more so than the diaries, a laboratory of the psyche. They are like dreams in which everyone in the dream is yourself, in one aspect or another. All these women were parts of Nin, and I recognized pieces of myself in all of them. The stories were seductive and fantastic, psychologically acute and glittered with their own intense inner life.

I think what attracted me most about Anaïs Nin was that her women were always struggling to break through into an authentic life, with their sexuality and their courage and their joy intact.

And clearly, at fourteen, and fifteen, and sixteen, that's what I wanted for myself, to become a woman intact that way. Funny, they used to use the word *intact* to mean virginal—so *intact* didn't mean authenticity, but this sort of sealed blankness, like a piece of paper kept clean so that a man could eventually write himself on it. But *intact* for me meant with all the portions of myself continuing to belong to myself. Alive in all the parts, in the imagination, in the erotic self, in relationships, your life for your own use and benefit. At the time, that's what Anaïs Nin meant to me.

Flash forward a few years. Now I was in college. After changing my major a few times, I settled on history, not only as a degree but as a profession. The historian uses a lot of the elements of fiction writing— the characters, the drama, the sweep of events. But you didn't have to expose your own vulnerabilities. You could footnote everything.

My studies led me to England, for a Junior year abroad. It was the first time in four years (it was a second Junior year) of being away from my college, which was very intense and tended to focus you very intently on your academic future. Being away was a bit like waking up from an intense, vivid dream.

I turned twenty-one that year. And the night before my twenty-first birthday, I woke up at about three in the morning, dead upright, and realized I wanted to be a writer. I didn't want the academic life, I wanted to LIVE in the most profound sense of the word. I wanted to experience life, that life that Anaïs Nin had written about all those years ago. In fact, when I pictured myself as a writer, that's exactly what I had in mind. Not Emily Dickinson, or Charlotte Brontë, or Sylvia Plath. For me, "being a writer" meant freedom and self-discovery, and a life lived in high key. It was the picture of that slight, otherworldly woman in her cape and eyelashes. That was a future I could look forward to.

When I decided I wanted to be a writer like Anaïs Nin, I had not written a story yet. I had an unpleasant experience the first time I tried, when I was nine, at the hands of another teacher—I didn't have much luck in my early education—so for me, as it was for Anaïs Nin, the declaration came first, the intention, and then the work followed.

There has been some controversy about Anaïs Nin since the days I read those diaries—artists fall into fashion and out again. Everyone likes to find the hero's clay feet—it's our uneasiness about having heroes. But I'm older now too; I've found sides of my own character which I don't like very much, either. I don't need my heroes to be flawless; in fact, I expect them to be riddled with flaws and contradictions—who doesn't have them?

But I've never lost my affection for the writer who was my first inspiration. Anaïs Nin didn't become a writer in a time when women regularly went their own way. She had to clear her own path, become a new kind of writer, a new kind of woman, and as a writer who started in the 1930s, she had to wait quite some time for an audience, for people to catch up to her. Luckily she saw that before she died. Some writers don't get that lucky.

And what about Nin today?

I think that nowadays women are not quite as focused on their perceptions as women. The results of those battles are everywhere, so profound and deep that it's fallen out of consciousness. My daughter cannot believe that when I was her age, I couldn't take print shop, or wear pants to school, that there were no female jockeys, cops, soldiers, airline pilots, mail carriers, firefighters, bus drivers, news anchors, politicians and damn few writers. And that it was routine for men to make statements about women, what we could or could not do, and it wasn't bizarre for a substitute teacher to stand in front of a class and say there are no women writers. Anaïs Nin was part of that change. She understood when she was complimented that she thought like a man, it wasn't a compliment—it was saying that a woman who thinks like a woman doesn't think at all. She demonstrated to a generation that a woman who thinks like a woman thinks a great deal, and writes things that hadn't been seen on the page before.

She taught a generation of writers that a woman's writing doesn't have to resemble that of a man to be serious, that serious writing comes out of those who take themselves seriously, that their ideas and their creative lives, even their erotic lives, can be seen from the point of view of subject, and not object.

I've done my little Anaïs Nin pilgrimages—I have a picture of the house where she grew up in New York, a three-story brownstone in the west 70s, in my office. I've been to the Gotham Book Mart, where the books she printed on her own press were sold.

And every day for the last fifteen years, I walk my dog in the hills in Silver Lake, where I live, and often pass a Japanese style mailbox at the crest of the hill, which I've known is the house where Anaïs Nin lived with Rupert Pole in the last years of her life. It's the house in the film, "Anaïs Observed." All you can see from the street is a long driveway going back into the trees. But it was a little tiny shrine, that mailbox, and I never went up that hill without stopping just to contemplate—this is where Anaïs Nin lived.

When I published my novel *White Oleander*, in which I think an Anaïs Nin lover can see the influence, I told the story to a radio interviewer who offered to put me in touch with Rupert Pole, Anaïs's second husband, who still lived in the house, and see if I could get to meet him and see the place.

And so one day, some thirty years after my first encounter with Nin on the page, I found myself walking down that driveway, and being let in by Rupert, a lovely man I recognized from photographs, who gave me a tour of the house.

It was smaller than I thought it would be, and made of very humble materials, concrete block and plywood and glass, but elegant in its simple, almost Japanese style, with the big view over the Silver Lake reservoir. There in the living room was the bed they had slept in, and he took me back to see her writing room, a simple, glass walled room that looked out into the shady front garden. Here was her typewriter, here was her room. And I had a thought that I sometimes do have, about living too late, not way too late, but just late enough to have missed whatever happened in the room just before I arrived. I could see Anaïs Nin walking through that room, elegant in a long skirt and a white shirt. It was a house set up for lovers, the bed right in the living room, though I think it could be partitioned off in a pinch, but very unconventional. It was small, and modern and casual—it made the other houses seem over-appointed, Victorian by comparison.

The charm of that day, sitting with Rupert, talking about Anaïs and their great love, the way she kept her journals, her relationships with her students, their circle of friends, will always stay with me like the closing of a circuit.

I always regretted having missed Anaïs Nin—she spoke at the commencement at my college shortly before I started; I was a high school student in Los Angeles at a time when she was very accessible to young people—but I suppose the challenge now is to renew the inspiration she embodied. Even thinking about her for this speech has rekindled my admiration, and I hope will inspire us all again to seek the high moments and continue searching for the miraculous. ❖

Rupert Pole in the Silver Lake house
Photo Yuko Yaguchi

Lynette Felber

A Heated Correspondence
Anaïs Nin and Rebecca West on writers' community

Т he publication of the first volume of Anaïs Nin's *Diary* in 1966 was long-anticipated—the *Diary* itself was legendary and so were its insider portraits of celebrated writers and bohemian avant-garde artists. The legal quagmire entailed in acquiring permission to publish the verbal "portraits" of Nin's numerous acquaintances and friends, however, was one of several logistical problems that delayed its publication for over thirty years. Although many writers were happy to have their portraits published, Rebecca West refused her permission to be featured in the *Diary*. The heated correspondence that followed foregrounds issues of interest to writers in general. An exchange of their letters housed in West's papers at the University of Tulsa highlights the two women's contrasting perceptions of writers' community. In their interchange, the two writers explore questions about what a writer owes fellow writers in terms of encouragement, promotion, and support, both personally and professionally. The writers reveal a variety of emotions elicited by this issue, including betrayal, anger, criticism, and disappointment over lack of support.

Anaïs Nin and Rebecca West knew each other both professionally and personally. West first encountered Nin's work when she reviewed *D.H. Lawrence: An Unprofessional Study*, published in 1932. The two writers finally met face-to-face during Nin's visit to New York in 1935. Later that year, West visited France and the two were reacquainted in Rouen (where West's son was at school). During this visit, West was a guest at Nin's home in Louveciennes, and she and her husband dined in Paris with the now infamous but then unacknowledged love trio of Nin, Hugh Guiler, and Henry Miller.[1] Nin admired West's "rich breasts, her gypsy skin, her ardent eyes, her humor and irony" (*Fire* 130). The women discovered that they had much in common besides their writing: both had charming, irresponsible fathers who had abandoned their families, a source of enduring trauma for each of them. Nin would probably not have differentiated between their personal and professional relationships; it is less certain that West would have blurred the boundaries of this distinction. However, Nin's plans to publish an account of their private, social meetings contributed to West's disenchantment with the friendship in the 1960s—subsequently leading her to ignore Nin's work professionally.

Nearly of the same generation—Nin was thirty-two and West forty-two when they met—the two women had markedly different careers. West got her start as a writer through her work as a young suffragette and a contributor to Doris Marsden's feminist publication *The Freewoman*. By the age of twenty, West was already publishing book reviews and her career as a critic was successfully launched. By 1947, she was featured on the cover of *Time* magazine as the world's number one woman writer, and she became a Dame of the British Empire in 1958. Nin, a part of a bohemian circle of writers and artists, had a slowly growing but loyal underground following of readers and fought for decades to be publicly recognized. West's reputation was bankable, and many of her novels were Book-of-the-Month Club selections. Nin's books were deemed "uncommercial" by publishers, and while Nin published her book on D.H. Lawrence in the 1930s, and a significant amount of fiction in the 1940s, she did not gain an international reputation among general readers until the late 1960s and early 1970s, with a meteoric rise to best-selling cult status after the publication of her diaries. These contrasting career trajectories—as well as two quite different personalities—contributed to their antithetical perceptions of a writer's duty to her fellow writers and to a community of writers. Nin's concept of the writers' community was facilitative and nurturing; West's was challenging and adversarial.

Nin depicts her early relationships with writers as a network of support: she wrote of Lawrence Durrell and Miller that "[w]e thought simply of enriching each other or giving the other the sustenance he needed, but we also felt that we were giving to each other. There was no idea of competition" (*Woman* 95). This account, written years after the fact, may be somewhat idealized, however. At the time of her affair with Miller, for example, Nin was gratified when West praised her writing at the expense of her lover's: "Rebecca definitely does not like Henry's writing. Thinks my preface to *Tropic of Cancer* a beautifully alive thing which bears no relation to the book. 'He has no vision,' she says" (*Fire* 131). Although a tinge of competition may stain all professional relationships, Nin's dealings with other writers were generally supportive rather than critical. Her long struggle for recognition convinced her that writers' camaraderie and solidarity were essential. When she finally achieved fame, Nin encouraged young writers who sought her support. After an early and disappointing attempted correspondence with Djuna Barnes in the 1930s, Nin had resolved to act differently: "Djuna Barnes could have answered my letter, as I am answering my mail today. And that is why I'm doing it. Because I thought it was unkind of her not to answer a beautiful letter about her work, about *Nightwood*" (*Woman* 101). Because she believed that "craft" would come in due time and was not necessarily taught (*Woman* 217), Nin supported other writers by reading and commenting favorably on their work rather than criticizing or editing. She also used her financial resources to serve as a patron to many writers, supplying rent money, a typewriter, a dinner—whatever would facilitate the writing process. She underwrote the publication of *Tropic of Cancer* for Miller in the 1930s (Stuhlmann xv), and when she and her friends found conventional publication difficult to achieve in the 1940s, Nin bought and operated a printing press in New York, producing hand-crafted, artistic books that are valuable collectors' editions today.

Throughout her career, Nin refused to differentiate between promotional writing on behalf of writers (of which she contributed her share) and professional reviews or criticism. Her "unprofessional" study of Lawrence was more of an appreciation than a critical analysis. She was often unhappy with scholars' criticism, though she approved of Evelyn Hinz's and Anna Balakian's approaches to her work. Nin either did not understand or simply could not sympathize with the professional critic's and reviewer's goals of objective analysis and honest evaluation. West, on the other hand, was a professional reviewer from the start. Her love affair with H.G. Wells was initiated by a jeering, provocative review of his novel *Marriage* in 1912, in which she publicly dubbed her future lover an "old maid among novelists" ("Marriage" 64). In this seemingly belittling review, West spoke the adversarial language of professional criticism that Wells understood. The review precipitated a relationship that began in 1913 and continued for ten years. West viewed the book review as a form which challenges in the interest of truth. In a 1952 article, she wrote: "A jog-trot review which questions facts is, if its questioning is on a proper basis, part of a scheme for stripping the earth of its wrapping of deceptive mists, which stripping can never be entirely successful but which should be made without cease lest those mists choke the human race" ("Art" 168). Nin reacted ambivalently to West's acerbic professional persona; she wrote: "Her tongue is sharp, and she does not suffer from naïveté. At her age, will I be as sharp? Her descriptions of people are merciless" (*Fire* 130). But Nin apparently saw a side of West that the critic did not often publicly reveal; Nin also wrote, "She is hypersensitive to criticism" (*Fire* 119), a statement that even better describes her own vulnerability.

West was particularly vulnerable because of her troubled relationship with her son by H.G. Wells, Anthony West. She not only asked to have any reference to herself deleted from the *Diary*, but she also reacted emotionally to Nin's alleged misinterpretation of West's previous comments about her son. In a typewritten letter to Nin dated

November 4, 1965, West says she will accept Nin's offer to strike the section about her from the published diary.[2] For her part, Nin wanted to retain the portrait and responded by offering West the option of editing the passage herself: "Take a red pencil... Can anything be kept?" (Tulsa, Nov. 13, 1965). She also wrote to ask West's opinion of the *Diary*, and when she did not receive a prompt answer (apparently because some correspondence was lost in the mail), Nin wrote West an angry letter communicating her sense of betrayal:

Dear Rebecca:

It was out of faith in our friendship that I wrote to you about the diary and offered to take out anything which displeased you. It was out of consideration for our friendship that I took out every reference to you. I awaited a long letter you said you wrote to me which never came. I wrote you that I had left you out entirely from the diary. I counted on your [word crossed out, "friendship"?] love and understanding in the past. I also remembered you as objective and generous. But when I wrote to you later and asked you: was there nothing in the diary you could comment on, nothing to admire, nothing to respond to, nothing you could recognize as you did in the past, you did not answer me. I cannot believe you can so deeply admire [in?] cold blood, preface, comment on so many books, and be silent about the diary in a way which annihilates your understanding in the past. If this is true, then I am free again of the bonds of friendship and can write about you in the coming diaries. I can also write that you relied on my noblesse oblige to write nothing at all, and yet failed utterly in noblesse oblige to give to the diary even a friend's response. I cannot believe this until you write me yourself. I cannot believe that what I may have written in my twenties, may have bothered you so much, that it turned you against me for good. If this is so I would like to know it. I have worked in the opposite direction: I have sought to find in the past the causes for breaks, alienations, so that I would not have to report in the diary anything bitter or distorted. There must be a reason for your attitude. It is not that of a friend. Before this new aspect of you represents the Rebecca West of today, I would like to give you an opportunity to break your silence of twenty years about my work. It is essential to me. For my loyalties do not change, but I know it is possible for others to change so utterly.

I hope I will find again the Rebecca West I knew, outspoken, loving, and generous.

(Tulsa, Nov. 23, 1966)

Nin's use of the phrase "*noblesse oblige*" seems idiosyncratic; clearly she uses the term to indicate an obligation of generous behavior—but an obligation grounded in friendship rather than that of social rank. A comment in *The Novel of the Future* further illuminates the personal meaning Nin attaches to this term: "People only unmask themselves in the privacy of love or friendship. But such revelations impose *noblesse oblige*. One has to treat them with care and tenderness. A human being who reveals himself should be treated with the same care we accord a new type of fish, a new type of plant. He is unique and we may never see another like him. We must protect him from injury if we are to share his life" (150). Self-revelation, Nin claims, creates a vulnerability that merits special protection. Nin obviously felt that West's refusal to let her publish the portrait betrayed their friendship, the bond created by that process of mutual self-revelation and resultant vulnerability. Their prior reciprocal emotional exchange necessitated, in Nin's view, not just an obligation to act generously with each other personally, but also as fellow writers, to read and comment on each other's work.

Another revealing usage in Nin's letter is her application of the word "objective" to West's prior behavior. Nin here seems to appeal to West's role as a professional book reviewer: if she can comment in "cold blood" on books by strangers, cannot she comment on the work of a friend? Nin elucidates her views on the traditional dichotomy between objective and subjective expression in a lecture transcribed in *A Woman Speaks*. Again, the personal and emotional dimension of writing means more to Nin than any kind of objective evaluation of books: "Because the source of our human life, the source of our personal happiness all the time depends on this personal world... The discovery I made from my own work was that while being accused of all these things in my twenties and in my thirties, of being subjective, of being only concerned with the personal world, I suddenly realized that when you went deeply enough into the personal you touched the sources of our human life and our humanity." Therefore, Nin goes on to explain, "I don't believe there is objective criticism... I did not write about Lawrence objectively" (*Woman* 86-87).

Book reviews, therefore, raised two sensitive issues for Nin: the personal obligation of one writer to another and the impossibility of objective criticism. She had no sympathy for either the antagonistic culture of the professional book review or the financial exigency of the commercial marketplace. In 1944, Nin observed that "I have met [...] with only one insuperable obstacle: the reviewers. They side with the commercial publishers. They will not review books by small presses unless these small presses...get themselves publicized" ("Anaïs Nin" 494).

Nin's sense of betrayal may have been fostered by some very positive early experiences with book reviews and reviewers. Reviewers who were friends (e.g. Edmund Wilson, who was also her lover), or who had connections with publishers, aided the publication of her work. Gore Vidal, for example, "fought" for publication of *Children of the Albatross* at Dutton, though their relationship deteriorated after Gore published parodic depictions of Nin in his novels (*Diary 4* 191). Nin received encouragement from many reviewer-friends—Wilson and West herself wrote favorable reviews of her early works. In 1932, West included Nin's *D.H. Lawrence: An Unprofessional Study* in her review of five books on Lawrence published in the London *Daily Telegraph*. West wrote that Lawrence "has been discussed more brilliantly and profoundly than ever before in a book by a lady with the fascinating name of Anaïs Nin, in a volume, written in English, though published by Titus in Paris... People who say that they cannot understand what Lawrence was after will find this last a very pleasant way of finding out" ("Hero-Worship" 6).[3] West genuinely admired Nin's work, but this statement also embodies the kind of un-analytic promotion Nin herself wrote and understood. West's review goes on to give much more extensive and critical treatment to a biography of Lawrence, *The Savage Pilgrimage: A Narrative of D.H. Lawrence* by Catherine Carswell; in comparison, her praise of Nin's study is merely an aside. West also praised Nin's *Winter of Artifice* some years later, and was quoted in print as saying "I think the whole thing quite marvelous, particularly in its use of absolutely new material. You seem to me to have real and unmistakable genius" (qtd. in "Anaïs Nin," 493).

In the 1966 letter to West, Nin expresses her dismay that West's early professional support had diminished and had been followed by a twenty-year silence. Clearly, Nin was looking for more than just permission to publish her portrait of West; her letter shows her seeking some commentary on the *Diary* as Nin's lifework. Deirdre Bair claims that West had not been willing to help Nin find a publisher for the diaries in England (214, 251, 564, n.5), and although Bair is an unsympathetic biographer whose depiction generally places Nin in the most unflattering light possible, her account in this case is supported by the veiled threat in Nin's 1966 letter. Nin intimates that if West violates the bonds of friendship, Nin will be free to publish what she pleases about West in future volumes. This interpretation of her letter is confirmed by volume two of the *Diary* (1934-39), in which a brief but highly factual portrait of West appears. In this volume, Nin provides a narrative account of their past encounters, including visits and West's prior positive review of Nin's book on Lawrence. Although Nin did retaliate, in one sense, by publishing the portrait, it was carefully edited and there is nothing objectionable or negative in it. She did not mention West's subsequent lack of cooperation (*Diary 2* 31-32), and a more detailed portrait of West was eventually published in the posthumous *Fire*, Nin's "unexpurgated" journal from 1934-37 (118-119, 129-134).

What West actually felt about the *Diary* as a literary work is unknown since she withheld any comment on the *Diary* itself. Her papers in the Tulsa collection also include a typed copy of Nin's story "Ragtime," which Nin probably sent for her comments, but which bears no annotations by West. In her correspondence with Gordon Ray, however, who consulted with West about a couples biography of her relationship with Wells, West made many bitter comments about Nin (Bair 563, n.32; 609, n.44; 654, n.5). For her part, Nin articulated ambivalence about West as early as 1936, when she wrote: "I love Rebecca, but she is too sick, too neurotic, too difficult as a friend" (*Fire* 213; also see 293). At the same time, West herself was less than candid (with Nin or with herself) about her own motivations. Her reluctance to let Nin publish her portrait was at least partially grounded in her obsessive efforts to keep her battle with her son out of print (Felber). She wrote Nin: "I certainly misled you if I gave you to understand that my son resented being illegitimate and hated me—and I shouldn't like him to think that I had told you this. Actually his attitude in those days was entirely different. He was proud and fond of his father, and certainly did not hate me. He was difficult, but the difficulty was quite of another kind, and much less ordered—much less definable" (Tulsa, Nov. 4, 1965). Still, Nin never published the material to which West most objected, revealing her son's hostility, in either the original or in the posthumous diaries. Evidently, Nin's sense of *"noblesse oblige"* (passed down to her executors) governed her choice of material, though she felt a right to select from it because West had breached the bond of friendship.

Nin's subjective, facilitative view of the function of book reviewers and writers' obligations to each other in contrast with West's more objective, adversarial one also informs Nin's and West's different kinds of feminism and their reputations among feminists today. Nin was suspicious of feminists who try to be "like men"; she wrote disapprovingly of Rebecca West (and Virginia Woolf) that "each write[s] like a man and I don't like it" ("Notes"; Bair 102). The exchange of letters in the Tulsa collection, as well as a comparison of Nin's and West's personal conduct in their relationship, suggests that what Nin meant when she accused West of writing "like a man" was, at least in part, West's willingness to adopt the adversarial position of the professional reviewer. Nin, in contrast, assumed a nurturing style of feminism, perhaps more acceptable in the late 1960s than today. Ironically, the reputations of both women have suffered in the contemporary feminist and academic communities. Nin is often denigrated for arguing that women are different from men, and has been accused of essentialism, though her belief that society's treatment of women needs to change shows that she did not believe that sex roles are truly "essential," that is, unchangeable and inherent. Similarly, West is criticized because she became more conservative as she grew older and is credited, at most, with a paradoxical feminism that departed from her early radical suffrage feminism by endorsing women's reliance upon the feminine mystique, including a more passive role in relation to men (Norton).

Throughout their lives in the volatile first three-quarters of the twentieth century, Nin and West stepped boldly through a minefield of women's shifting roles and evolving professional identities. Their rift in the 1960s reflects not only their personal biases about book reviews and the writer's duty to fellow writers, but also foreshadows some of the differences that characterize contemporary debates in feminist communities today.◈

Rebecca West

Works cited

"Anaïs Nin." *Current Biography: Who's News and Why*. Ed. Anna Rothe. New York: H.W. Wilson, 1944.

Bair, Deirdre. *Anaïs Nin: A Biography*. New York: Putnam, 1995.

Felber, Lynette. "Unfinished Business: Rebecca West's Aborted Novel, *Mild Silver, Furious Gold.*" *Journal of Modern Literature.* Forthcoming.

Fitch, Noel Riley. *Anaïs: The Erotic Life of Anaïs Nin.* Boston: Little, Brown, 1993.

Nin, Anaïs. *The Diary of Anaïs Nin, Vol. 2, 1934-1939.* Ed. and preface Gunther Stuhlmann. New York: Harcourt, 1967.

----. *The Diary of Anaïs Nin, Vol. 4, 1944-1947.* Ed. and introd. Gunther Stuhlmann. New York: Harcourt, 1967.

----. *Fire: From "A Journal of Love." The Unexpurgated Diary of Anaïs Nin, 1934-1937.* Ed. Gunther Stuhlmann. New York: Harcourt, 1995.

----. "Notes on Feminism." *Massachusetts Review* 13.1 & 2 (1972): 25-28.

----. *The Novel of the Future.* New York: Collier, 1968.

----. *A Woman Speaks: The Lectures, Seminars, and Interviews of Anaïs Nin.* Ed. and introd. Evelyn J. Hinz. Chicago: Swallow, 1975.

Norton, Ann V. *Paradoxical Feminism.* Lanham: International Scholars P, 2000.

Rollyson, Carl. *Rebecca West: A Life.* New York: Scribner's, 1996.

Stuhlmann, Gunther ed. "Introduction." *A Literate Passion: Letters of Anaïs Nin and Henry Miller 1932-1953.* San Diego: Harcourt, 1987.

West, Rebecca. "The Art of Skepticism." *Vogue* Nov. 1, 1952, 114-115, & 167-168.

----. "Hero-Worship of D.H. Lawrence." *Daily Telegraph* June 24, 1932: 6. col. 3-5.

----. "Marriage." Rev. of *Marriage* by H.G. Wells. Rpt. in *The Young Rebecca: Writings of Rebecca West 1911-17.* Ed. and introd. Jane Marcus. Bloomington: Indiana UP, 1982. 64-69.

Notes

[1] Their visits are described in detail in *Fire*: 89; 118-119; 129-133. Nin's and West's biographers also describe their visits; see Fitch, 182; Rollyson, 170; and Bair, 213-214.

[2] This letter and those subsequently quoted are housed in the largest collection of West's papers in the McFarlin Library at the University of Tulsa. I gratefully acknowledge the Anaïs Nin Trust as well as a travel-to-collection grant I received from *Tulsa Studies in Women's Literature* that made examination of these materials possible.

[3] My thanks to the document delivery staff at Indiana University-Purdue University Fort Wayne—particularly Mark Schobert, Christine Smith, and Cheryl Truesdell—for locating this elusive document.

Kazuko Sugisaki

Translating Anaïs Nin's *Incest* into Japanese
Inciting the eye of a Yin woman

I shall begin with a story.

One fine day you are invited to a castle on the top of a mountain, and given a tour of the place. It is a beautiful castle built of marble, colorful tiles, and glass. It has several towers, countless rooms, windows and doors. Mirrors are everywhere. Fires are burning in fireplaces. One staircase leads you underground. There you find intricate labyrinths in which you are almost trapped. You are told that a woman has built this castle, all alone, devoting all her life to it. You are awed by its splendor.

"I wonder if you could build another castle just like this, an exact replica, in a foreign land," a voice says. "I'll give you one hundred dollars for the work." Of course, you could say, "No," and flatly decline the ridiculously unrealistic offer. But, there is something irresistible about the tone of the voice, and besides, you are so fascinated by the castle. You think and hesitate, but finally decide that maybe you have the ability to do it. So you say, "Yes, I'll try my best."

Now, it turns out that in the foreign land where the new castle is to be constructed none of the material used for the original can be obtained. So you have to use some ordinary stone instead of marble, paper instead of glass. You have a lot of other things to use—rocks, pebbles, wood, bamboo, sea-plants, flower petals. You work desperately hard and since you are a good craftsperson, one day the castle is complete. It looks just like the original and is just as intricate and beautiful. The only problem is that you know it is *not* the exact replica of the original.

This is precisely what I am experiencing translating Anaïs Nin's *Incest* into Japanese. It is an enormous project. The book is four hundred and three pages thick, and it demands that I pay very scrupulous attention to every detail of it in terms of meaning, ideas, expression, and the harmony of the whole. Very often while crafting this and that I find myself lost in Nin's unending labyrinths.

Translation of literature is hard work! It requires time, effort, persistence, perseverance, patience, literary sensitivity, and above all, you yourself must be an artist to create literature in the receptor language. In the end, your work brings you neither fame nor money.

Then why do you do it? Why do you spend months, years sometimes, laboring over someone else's artwork, trying to transform it into another language? It seems such an unrewarding labor. You do it, I suppose, just for the love of it. You read a particular work of literature, and you fall in love with it. You feel you understand it well enough to want to share the experience with someone else, with those around you, and with many others who don't know the original language. You also admire the writing style so much that you are tempted to re-create it in your own language. It is a challenge, a tormenting, yet enjoyable and exciting challenge.

There is something very different in translating English into Japanese from that into any of the European languages. First of all, letters we use are worlds apart. One word Nin is obsessed with, *love*, becomes *ai* (愛) in Japanese. It does not look anything like French *amour*, or German *libe*, does it? I feed the word *shoka* to the machine. It is another favorite word of Nin's. Very faithfully the computer gives 47 possible choices. Depending on the characters you use for the same pronunciation, meanings are totally different. It can mean digestion (消化), fire extinguishing (消火), children's song (唱歌), department of business (商科), merchant (商家), and forty-two other things. With Nin, it is always this *shoka* (昇華)—sublimation. (After repeating the conversion process thousands of times, one evening, my computer refused to do the job!)

And there is the problem of *I* and *you*. There are countless ways of saying *I* and *you* in the Japanese language depending on the speaker's gender, age, social status, occasions, situations, etc. It is obvious that Anaïs's *I* (*watakushi* = 私) should be different from Henry's *I* (*boku* = 僕). But should Henry's *I* be different from Hugo's? What about Anaïs's father's *I* and Rank's? Should it be an imposing *I* for father or gentle and humble? By choosing a particular *I* for a particular person, we can almost define his or her character.

In the episode in which Allendy proposes flogging Anaïs, he says, "...Henry hasn't beaten you, has he? I'm going to possess you as you never have been possessed. You devil."[1]

Mocking and slighting *you* (*omae* = お前) in this case certainly should be different from admiring and endearing *you* (*anata* = あなた) when Rank uses it:

"I have been looking for a name for you," I (Anaïs) said.
"I, too," said Rank, "and I can only think of YOU. When I say YOU, you stand before me."[2]

Let me give you a short sample of translation. Believe it or not, (A) and (B) are the same. The word order, too, is quite different.

(A)

Not Father, not Henry, nobody can really follow me all the way, understand me completely, accompany me. My journal and I. I have been again too feminine. Today I feel hard and strong and alone. So alone it frightens me. I am in every way such a fool. A lonely fool.[3]

(B)

　父もヘンリーも、私を完全に理解することはないし、私と一緒に目的地まで歩いてはくれない。私と日記だけ。今までの私は女性的でありすぎた。これからは独りで立つ。たった独りで、しっかりと立つ。その孤独が恐ろしくもある。何処から見ても私は立派な馬鹿だ。淋しい馬鹿だ。

(Father ＝ 父, I＝私, understand ＝ 理解する, completely ＝ 完全に, journal ＝ 日記, alone ＝ 独り, fool ＝ 馬鹿.)

One of the main issues of literary translation is whether a translation should read as a contemporary of the original or as that of the translator. If, for instance, Shakespeare is read and spoken in 17th Century Japanese, our contemporary audience would have a hard time understanding him. On the other hand, the text must give some texture, some flavor that indicates its origin.

What I feel to be unique and remarkable characteristics of Nin's writing style is that, even though most of *Incest* was written in the early 1930s, it is amazingly modern. Translating it seventy years later, I have no concerns whether or not faithful reconstruction of any Nin passages may sound too archaic.

It is because, perhaps, she writes almost exclusively about her inner world where her own private climate prevails, the climate whose air is charged with the psychological, the emotional, and the sensual. Kissing, caressing, desire, joy, exaltation, understanding, jealousy, hurt, and love. All of us understand love as love, sexual ecstasy as sexual ecstasy, spiritual and emotional hunger as exactly that. Time does not lay any patina on them.

And her language is direct and strong, using terms that describe what is happening right then and there.

About her affair with Father, Nin writes:

Ecstatic, his face, and I now frenzied with the desire to unite with him…undulating, caressing him, clinging to him. His spasm was tremendous, of his whole being. He emptied all of himself in me…and my yielding was immense, with my whole being, with only that core of fear, which arrested the supreme spasm in me.[4]

Take one moment and consider *The Tale of Genji*, a long novel written by a woman in the 11th Century. The very crucial scene of the first love union between the Prince Genji and his young protégé, Princess Murasaki, is described simply: The princess stayed in bed late this morning.

For someone like me born and raised in a culture whose literature traditionally relies heavily on images of natural beauty to describe the tangible and the intangible, on creating images to hint, to suggest, it is somewhat strange to realize that not even one flower is mentioned in the four hundred and three pages of *Incest*. There, no pine trees sway, no moon reflects on a quiet pond, no clouds announce approaching storms that might mow down pampas grasses and violate the pristine garden of the palace. *The Tale of Genji* is full of symbolism of this kind. The land where I intend to transplant Nin is indeed a very different place. And there is a danger that the translated text could meet a cool, impassive reception.

Times are changing, however, and we have women writers who write with braver, bolder and more direct strokes. One writer, Takako Takahashi, comes to mind as having Nin-like qualities. I quote below short passages I selected and translated from her work.

What interests me most of all is me, myself who have been hurt and unhappy. Ever since I can remember, I have been concerned with myself, watching and observing my unhappy self.[5]

This is perfect, at least something close to perfection, just being here now, like this… It is true that I love this man, but what I am waiting for is my own desire that reaches me through this man. Carried by this desire, from the deepest depth of myself, an unmanageable strange woman appears. It is a woman much thicker than my ordinary self, almost a mad woman, naked, violent, voracious, simple as a killer, gathering in herself the life that is too full. It is a woman strange to me, yet I feel I have known her all my life, no, not all my life, even before I was born. If I ask her, "Who are you?" the woman would reply, "I am you."

This is the person I really love, Michiko thought. But to meet this woman Michiko had to sleep with a man.[6]

I want to destroy Sister Sasaki, Yayoi thought. I want to expose that fresh wound hidden under her black nun's attire, make it bleed again. Imagining the nun screaming with pain, Yayoi felt excitement, exaltation. The hunger I have could be connected with this imagined sensation.[7]

"You have immense hunger for something, don't you?" asked the nun.
Yayoi didn't say anything, but she realized that she had had this unbearable hunger, thirst all her life. In the past, to pour water into her burning throat was the only reason for her to live, and it will be also for this reason that she will live in the future.[8]

These short quotations hardly do justice to Takahashi's voluminous writing, but I hope even they could incite some literature lovers in America to translate her delicate yet deeply complex work into English.

Anaïs Nin represents to me a Yang woman who had walked in light all her life. Being a Yang woman, she has that tiny black eye with which she can see into the heart of a Yin woman, her Japanese counterpart. The Japanese Yin woman may be still in a shadow, but she too has the small white eye with her. And that eye may sparkle with excitement when she reads Anaïs Nin.

When Ezra Pound published *Cathay* in 1915, his translation of Li Po poems, he hardly knew Chinese. But the poetry he recreated was so superb that it was received with tremendous enthusiasm. T.S. Eliot called Pound "the inventor of Chinese poetry" because "through his translation we really at last get the original."[9]

By no means do I claim to be the inventor of the Nin *Diary*, but at least I hope to be her Japanese shaman, the woman through whom Nin's spirit speaks. ◈

Notes

---

[1] Nin, Anaïs, *Incest*. New York: Harcourt Brace Jovanovich, 1992. 147.

[2] Ibid. 339.

[3] Ibid. 275.

[4] Ibid. 209.

[5] Takahashi, Takako. "Going into My Self." Tokyo: *Waseda Bungaku*, Waseda University, July 1976. 83.

[6] Takahashi. *Waste Land*. Tokyo: Kawadeshobo Shinsha, 1980. 156-157.

[7] Ibid. 120.

[8] Ibid. 66.

[9] Eliot, T.S. ed. "Introduction." *Ezra Pound: Selected Poems*. London: Faber & Gwyer, 1928. 14.

Anaïs Nin in Japan, 1966
Photo © Anaïs Nin Trust

Daisy Aldan

Flight

I have lost the visitations of angels
across my heart. You have joined the ring
on the other side of the mist where
stark and angular phantoms hover.
There is sand in the flower pot—and a dry stalk.
   I can unfasten my seat belt now
   and start smoking. Hieroglyphics
   scrawl FINIS across the snow-covered
planes of Utah, over the Rockies, past the golden
   desert where I, dauntless pioneer,
   sought you, and when you refused to be IT,
   died in California, in a glass
booth on an empty street near a garage
   where the western sun cast no shadow.
   Your filtered voice, a hypodermic
   needle in an open heart, bleeding.
It was my last gasp. You ceased to become. Finding
   no path through the mountains, I chartered
   a Jet East, and was carried, winding
   across a sky like a cracked mirror,
into the ice cube land. The wind roared and frost
   whitened wings and framed windows. We swerved
   upwards, seeing always the same curve
   of lights, red and blue, the arrows
pointing in two directions, and the tower.
   But there's an oxygen mask and a life
   vest; and as birds know when to gather
   for flight, my heart may revive at midnight.

Paul Herron

An Afternoon with Joaquín Nin-Culmell
The composer's life today

oaquín Nin-Culmell's house is set in a pristine neighborhood in Oakland, California, and it faces the same direction that the houses in Louveciennes and Silver Lake do—west. They catch the brilliant sun in the latter part of the day, the light pouring through the windows and illuminating the most prominent rooms. The exterior of the house is very well kept, a light gray plaster with white, ornate wooden trim. It is April, and the flowers are in bloom, the grass green in the small yard.

We approach the door, which is half-hidden behind a semi-circle canopy. As I ring the doorbell, I say to my wife Sara, "I cannot believe how nervous I am." We are, after all, about to meet the last living member of the Nin family, a composer whose name is known worldwide.

The door opens. A young man, Joaquín's assistant, greets us and welcomes us inside. As we enter, I feel that we are treading hallowed turf. I look to the left and see the piano room—white, elegant, airy, its centerpiece the grand piano set before windows adorned by fine blinds, through which the bright mid-afternoon light enters. To the right, just around the corner, we get a glimpse of Joaquín. We tentatively step into the small room, which serves as a sitting and eating area, recognizing it as the very place Joaquín sat for a BBC documentary[*] some nine years ago. He turns around to look at us. He wears large glasses, not thick, an informal knit shirt. His face is angelic. His fine features are highlighted by his swept-back white hair, and his smile is infectious. For a man in his nineties, he looks marvelous. His skin is smooth and soft-looking. His voice is that of a much younger man. He is very affable, if not a wee bit wary, which is understandable since he only knows me from the telephone.

He invites us to sit down and asks if we want something to drink. We decline, and he says, "Even juice??" "We just had something to drink," Sara says, and he laughs at this, saying, "Oh, I see. You had something to *drink*." The afternoon is beginning with levity and humor. I immediately begin to feel relief and to relax.

---

[*] *See pg. 154 for more information*

Sara comments on how beautiful the house is. "Oh, I bought the house from my mother." He says she spent some of her last days here. It seems that of the family, the mother could only count on Joaquín— his older brother Thorvald had moved away, his older sister Anaïs was living her intense life, and her husband by then had been long gone.

Thorvald: He was the "non-artist" in the family, the one to whom his father once scoffed, "The only reason I brought you into the [world] was to get to Joaquín, the musician." Thorvald hated his father, and he eventually grew apart from the entire family. He became an engineer, worked and lived in Columbia, Venezuela and Mexico, first in oil and then in plywood. He did well for himself. "I am surprised he didn't hate me," Joaquín says. "After all, I was the 'artist'." He adds, though, that Thorvald offered to give their mother the down payment for the house, and when the money arrived, she was surprised to see that it was for the full amount. "He was generous," Joaquín says, "generous and kind." He says he doesn't know why Thorvald had a falling out with Anaïs. "Thorvald didn't like Anaïs's boyfriends," Joaquín says with a smile. "Anaïs did not have good judgment when it came to men. Some of them were pretty goofy...except *Hugo*. He, Thorvald liked—we all did. He was a beautiful man." Joaquín goes on to say that Hugo was a "much greater literary influence for Anaïs than people think." I tell him how I'd read about Hugo's efforts to correct and enhance Anaïs's English, his admonishments for her use of strange and old-fashioned words. Joaquín nods emphatically.

"Anaïs was a kind sister, good to her siblings," he says. "She'd make us read various books, you see, like big sisters do, and then we'd have to explain to her what we'd read."

Thorvald was, and remains, an enigma. Joaquín, however, is close to Thorvald's daughter, Gail Rosenkrantz. I recall she seemed bitter about Anaïs's failings as an aunt, and reporting that Thorvald thought Anaïs's French accent was "phony."[*] Joaquín claims there was nothing phony about the accent.

We ask about Louveciennes. He tells us that he lived in the house there during the thirties, up until such time when his mother decided she did not want him "riding trains all the time" back and forth to Paris, where he studied at the *Conservatoire*, near Gare St-Lazare. His mother took an apartment nearby so that he could simply walk to his lessons. Henry Miller attended Joaquín's first recital in Paris and afterwards sent a letter to him saying, "You cannot play Schumann until you visit a whorehouse," which Joaquín laughs about now, but felt pain then, as

---

[*]*See* Recollections of Anaïs Nin by her Contemporaries *(Ed. Benjamin Franklin V, Ohio University Press, 1996), pp. 1-6.*

"a youngster who had just given his first public performance." However, he felt he'd performed "well enough to continue," and toured parts of Europe, including Spain. As for Miller, Joaquín says his letter demonstrated that he was "a typical German Romantic, the type that has to *experience* everything in order to write, create art, compose music." Then he adds, "I avoided reading anything he did until later in life, and when I did, I thought to myself, 'What do people *see* in him?' He was simply a bad writer, and a sad sack, I'm afraid." Joaquín and his mother left Paris for New York in 1938 as the atmosphere of war thickened. His mother felt he would have a much better chance of a career there than in pre-war Europe.

After arriving in New York, he was offered a job teaching at Williams College in Williamsburg, MA. He says, "I don't know why they hired me, to tell you the truth. There is nothing worse than teaching when you don't know anything. It gets better when you *think* you know something." Laughter. He remained at Williams for ten years, whereupon the Dean told him, "You are too gifted to teach here at such a small college" and referred him to Berkeley, where he has been ever since. "I have loved it here," he says. This is easy to see…his house is a happy house, still reverberating from his brilliant career as a highly respected teacher and composer. "I loved it here because I could do what I damned well pleased!"

He maintains connections with the university, and oftentimes students or even accomplished professionals will come over and play for him. He affirms he gives criticism when asked, explaining, "They ask for my criticisms because I don't tell them any stories."

He no longer plays the piano or composes due to severe eye trouble. He went Barcelona a couple years ago to help audition performers for an opera he'd just written when suddenly things went dark. He asked someone if there was a terrible storm that had blackened the sky. He had gone blind. The doctors told him that they could not fix what was wrong. Although he has had some success with treatment here, he does not see well enough to play or compose.

We discuss Deirdre Bair's biography on Anaïs. He tells us that Bair actually spent weeks with him to gather information while she was researching the book, and that they got on quite well. I mention the controversy surrounding the book, that many Nin supporters find it judgmental. "She is not nearly judgmental as *I* am," he says. I admit to him that I use the biography since it contains a reasonably accurate collection of names, dates, places, and so on. He looks at me, his eyes open wide, and says, "And *that* is what a biography is *for*, isn't it?"

I recall someone telling me how badly *Incest* affected Joaquín when it came out, how that at a conference in 1994 he told several of

Anaïs's "friends" that they didn't "know her at all." In the BBC documentary, Joaquín says that Anaïs's passages concerning her incestuous relationship with her father may have been the result of her psychiatrist's suggestion that she "write it all out, the fantasy, that is, as a form of therapy." He carries an everlasting and strong love for Anaïs, and he is intensely protective of her, but he seems to contradict himself with his defense of the Bair biography. Sensitive to how deeply conflicted he is about all this, I decide to spare him any more questions.

He gets up to show us around the house, pointing out some of the artwork he has. He doesn't walk quickly, but he gets around with the help of his cane with much enthusiasm. His voice reveals excitement in giving us a little tour. He shows us the large painting that faces the table at which we were sitting. It is of oriental characters, and after close inspection, Joaquín correctly identifies it to us. He then leads us into his bedroom, which is the last room to the right in the hallway that divides the house lengthwise. In the room, he has a large, beautiful portrait of his father taken, he says, in Havana when he was seventy. I've seen the photo before in one of Anaïs's diaries. "You can see what a lady-killer he must have been, can't you?" Joaquín asks. There are several portraits of his mother. One, taken in Cuba before she married, reveals a delicate-looking woman with large eyes. There is a second photo taken after the marriage, in a gown and turn-of-the-century hairdo, and another which is "her last passport photo," probably taken in the forties or early fifties. In this photo she looks aged and tired. It is obvious how much Joaquín adored his mother—she was his biggest supporter, and I get the impression she devoted herself to him until the end of her days. There also is a photo of young Joaquín, probably seven or eight years old, taken in Richmond Hill, New York. He was such an adorable-looking child, although Anaïs claims in her childhood diaries that she never saw him with toys that hadn't been destroyed.

Sara asks how his father influenced his music. "He didn't influence me because he didn't even know about my playing until I was in my late teens, and by then it was too late." He laughs. "I began playing because my mother needed someone to accompany her singing, that's how it all began. My father, though, no. When I played in Havana, he didn't even bother to show."

In the meantime, he is showing us all these photos, identifying all of them correctly. He takes us back into the sitting area. There is a ray of sunlight coming through the window, illuminating Joaquín's head. He asks again if we want juice. This time we accept, and his assistant brings us all something to drink. I get up to look around the piano room and discover a couple more photos there, one of Anaïs later in life, looking up and smiling at the sky, and another of what at first appears to be a sad-eyed, dark-haired little girl, dressed in a dark outfit collared by white lace, but Joaquín says it is he, explaining how such clothing was common in photos then. "That picture was taken shortly before we left Barcelona for New York," he says. "Boy, I was too *serious*, wasn't I?" referring to his somber look. Sara thinks he resembles some of Anaïs's early photos, in which she too is very "serious" looking.

All of this leads me to ask some questions about Joaquín's sight and his future. It may seem odd to be asking a man his age about his future, but Joaquín's vitality and youthful vigor make it perfectly reasonable. I ask how he composed. "Well, I went about it the wrong way," he says, looking back on his beginnings. "I sketch the music first on paper. I look at it and look at it, and then I add things, delete things, change things that aren't right. I keep changing things until they are the way I want them to be. I write the music, the orchestration, the arrangement, all before I play it. I see it all up here first," he says, pointing to his head, "long before I ever use these," he concludes, wiggling his fingers, his fine, little fingers on small hands.

I ask if he has one of his music sheets handy, and he tells me to look in the music room by the piano. "I hope you don't mind," I say, "I cannot help myself—it's the scientist in me." "Oh no, by all means," he replies. I bring in a couple sheets and lay them out in front of him. They are illuminated by the gooseneck lamp he seems to always have on. He says, "Oh yes, I know this." He reads the name of the song, in Spanish, reads the initials of the composer, and some of the lyrics. The writing is faint and small. Then, I try my experiment. I ask for a piece of paper and a dark marker. I make the lines on the paper and write some notes in bold and large strokes. I ask if he can read it. "Well, actually yes, but I'm not so sure that it would work. Perhaps. Composing, that's the key all right, to my sadness. Yes. That is it." When one has acquired habits that span more than three quarters of a century, it must be very difficult to change, so I understand his hesitancy. Still, while we are talking, I have this nagging feeling to write a message at the bottom of the sheet. It is almost as though Anaïs is asking me to. So I write, "For Joaquín, to make music!"

Sara reminds me about the gift we have brought him—a gigantic huckleberry chocolate kiss—so I run out to the car to fetch it. We give it to Joaquín and his first reaction is that he can't eat chocolate (or drink wine, for that matter), but upon inspecting the huge candy, he becomes fascinated with it and says, "Well, I'll give it a go, and if it doesn't agree with me, I'll give it to [a friend], and if *he* doesn't like it, he can give it to his wife and three kids." We laugh.

It is time to go…we've been with him far longer than we hoped for. Joaquín seems as though he could keep going for some time—he is enjoying himself, saying, "You know, this is one of the few visits I've had that has been pleasurable. It seems that we agree on some of the things we *like*, and perhaps on some of those we *don't* like. Well, maybe 'don't like' isn't the right way to say it…but we do agree on some important points." Joaquín walks us to the door, shakes our hands, telling us, "This visit was a prize-winner." ◈

Joaquín Nin-Culmell
Photo © Sky Blue Press

Benjamin Joplin

A Problem to Be Solved:
Deleuzian becoming and Anaïs Nin's dream of "what ought to be"

I invoke Gilles Deleuze because I think it's time we revisit his philosophy in terms of the linkages it might make with Anaïs Nin's work. Far from blandly "applying" Deleuze to Nin and then culling a laundry list of "Deleuzian" passages from her work, space is better served here by outlining some of Deleuze's difficult literary theory, which we might then bear in mind for future Nin reading. Space is limited; the outline is broad. But it is broad enough to build Deleuze-Nin "assemblages" in some of our minds, at least temporarily. This essay is not meant to prove or disprove an existing relationship between them, but to make one.

I want to first attempt to rethink the implications of Nin's classic position on realism. I offer the claim that Nin championed a "symbolic" form of writing only *because of* (not in spite of) her aversion to the realists, and that once the kind of realism Nin disliked had had its day, as it were, Nin may well have abandoned all reference to (for her) existing, albeit overlooked, dreamlike and surrealistic worlds—the very worlds Nin-camp antirealists would celebrate. It is important to distinguish between a) the view that Nin championed only the kind of writing that would properly represent reality in ways realism did or could not, and b) the view that Nin ultimately did not argue for an alternate representation but for a literary philosophy that was *neither* symbolic nor representational at all. This latter view is mine.

In considering a nonrepresentational literary philosophy, I will place Nin in critical dialog with the French philosopher Gilles Deleuze. Both thinkers shared an abiding interest in Proust, Artaud, and Miller, among others. I will return to the question of "realism" as it is conceived by Nin, but before doing so, I will outline—broadly, very broadly—what a Deleuzian understanding of literature looks like. This particular outline comes from Daniel W. Smith, one of the translators of Deleuze's *Essays Critical and Clinical*. Smith lists "five interrelated effects" that can be said to characterize modern literature. My supplement to Smith's explanation of the literary Deleuze is in thinking of these five effects as de-essentializing movements. That is, Deleuzian thought is characterized as a flight from firm identities or essences so that he earns the title of philosopher of *becoming* rather than *being*. The first three effects are clearly iconoclastic: the Destruction of the World, the Dissolution of the Subject, and the Disintegration of the Body. The next two are related to the former three but are less directly de-essentializing: the Minorization of Politics and the Stuttering of Language.[1]

The first effect is the Destruction of the World, and the world at issue is a transcendent one, a *pre-existing reality* up to which narratives must measure (Smith xvii). For example, take the story of Adam and the Fall, which contains what Deleuze calls "singularities" such as "to be the first man" or "to sin" (Smith xv). There are "actualities" that these sets of word-signs represent, but such singularities obscure a host of possible "virtualities" that have potential as well. Deleuze wants to "free the virtual from its actualizations and [allow] it to assume a validity of its own" (Smith xv) so that the story becomes less about *actual* singularities and more about *virtual* ones—"to resist temptation," for instance. We needn't pit the actual against the virtual; we can also create new worlds by organizing them like a rhizome, by connecting one singularity to the next in a "multiplicity." Thus the unchanging transcendent World is destroyed as it becomes something other than what it was.

The second effect is the Dissolution of the Subject. The subject cannot exist in transcendence either because no one subject—not even Adam—has an essence. Instead of saying "we are all the same underneath contingent differences," Deleuze says subjects themselves are multiplicities. For example, Antonin Artaud, Deleuze notes, was not self-"defined by identity but by the process of 'becoming'" (Smith xxix). Instead, Artaud said, "I, Antonin Artaud, am my son, my father, my mother, and myself."[2]

Artaud carries us into the third effect, the Disintegration of the Body. It was Artaud who inspired Deleuze (and Deleuze's sometimes co-author Félix Guattari) to herald the Body Without Organs (BwO).[3] Because of limited space, BwO is a concept without too many ripples in this essay, unlike the rest of the effects. But note the BwO's relationship to the previous effect. In order to willfully disintegrate, one must extend to the body the same de-essentialization; do not limit "life" to an organic unity; rather, extend life's intensities in "lines of flight" from the body *out of the subject*. Deleuze and Guattari write, "Artaud wages struggle against the organs, but at the same time, what he's going after, what he has it in for, is the organism" (158). Without a BwO, the organism is limited in its self-containment. It needs a BwO to make assemblages—or, more specifically "desiring machines"—with the rest of the world.

In the fourth effect, the "Minorization of Politics," Deleuze makes strange the concept of minority, which here does not denote a representative of some already oppressed group but *"is itself a becoming or a process*, in constant variation, and the power of a minority is not measured by its ability to enter and make itself felt within the majority system" (Smith xliii, his emphasis). Recall that in the 1930s Nin was alienated by Gonzalo Moré's conception of politics, just as she was by the feminist movement of the 1960s and 1970s. Nin preferred not to affect political change by representing the wishes of a group for which they stand (women) but by actualizing "a creative storytelling that is, as it were, the obverse side of the dominant myths and fictions, an act of resistance whose political impact is immediate and inescapable, and that creates a line of flight on which a minority discourse and a people can be constituted" (Smith xlv).[4]

Finally, we have the "Stuttering of Language," wherein that very creativity is effected by a kind of "stuttering" rather than impeded by it. Stuttering is also a "minor" use of language because it operates by "taking any linguistic variable—phonological, syntactical or grammatical, semantic—and placing it in variation, following the virtual line of continuous variation that subtends the entire language" (Smith l-li). Deleuzians call it stuttering; Nin readers might call it "musicality."

Deleuze, as we can see, was interested not in language that approximates reality but language that creates or actualizes it from the pool of virtual possibilities. He writes that "Actualization breaks with resemblance as a process no less than it does with identity as a principle... In this sense, actualization or differentiation is always a genuine creation... For a potential or virtual object, to be actualized is to create divergent lines which correspond to—without resembling—a virtual multiplicity. The virtual possesses the reality of a task to be performed or a problem to be solved..."[5] Problem-solving creation is not returning to square one, "becoming is not an evolution[;]...the term we would prefer...is 'involution', on the condition that involution is in no way confused with regression... [T]o involve is to form a block that runs its own line 'between' the terms in play..." (*TP* 238-239). Indeed, if there was anything Anaïs Nin feared, it was regression and stagnation.

This brings us back to Nin and the question of realism and reality by way of a question for review: what was this "realism" that Nin found so hideous? The best explanation comes from *The Novel of the Future*, in which she asserts that it is the *familiar* that, "because it is familiar...we say it is real. But familiarity may be a façade, not reality."[6] It is the familiar that we take as literal, as "real" and "objective," and thus well-suited for realist fashion. It is the "poetic" or the "symbolic" that strives for unfamiliarity, or at least works *as* or *with* unfamiliarity in order to say something new about the mundane. Realists missed so much, she wrote—why did they forsake the dreams of the "inner" world for the grit and dirt of concrete objects, objects which represented nothing but themselves?

The problem that inspires this article is whether Nin conceived worlds as a matter of choice or privilege or as a matter of dissolution and creation. It would seem the former, but I suspect the latter. Choosing to celebrate the "inner" world, Nin certainly invested in representation, even if it corresponded to another, overlooked, world. But perhaps Nin employed the concept of "symbolism" *only as far as it could help represent something realism did not.*

We can trace Nin's antirealism to her personal need to find sanctuary from the "outer" world ("reality"). In a section from *The Novel of the Future* entitled "A spade is a spade is a spade is a spade," Nin complained that "[b]y a process which I am not equipped to analyze, American literature becomes the most literal, the most one-dimensional in the world" (*NF* 11). Nin needed symbolism as a *representational* wedge against the realists; she needed reference to the ignored other dimensions and thus still valued representation that might acknowledge them.

Realism wasn't just bad writing to be shrugged off; it served as a constant reminder that most people did *not* live within, or at least draw strength from, the "inner" world, which would also serve as the set and setting for Nin's work. Kim Krizan observes "a tension...for Nin between accuracy and illusion," one that spoke to a specific *modus operandi* of Nin's pen. Krizan says that "[t]his is the difference between simply recording information, chronicling events, thoughts, and feelings, and creating a world and a life in which she could be happy."[7] Beatrice Formentelli points out a related tension that parallels this inner/outer dichotomy; namely, that in "the prime of life" (about 1946), Nin was torn between "the dream" and "concrete reality," between escaping and affirming real life.[8] At this time, Formentelli says, Nin exhibited "two contradictory impulses: one, a deep-rooted urge to escape ugliness and pain through art or through the dream...the other her passionate compulsion to offer herself to the real world—and the real world...was that of people" (Formentelli 79). She then cites this passage from Nin's *Diary*: "What ought to be, not what is, interests me... In between, an all-consuming loneliness."[9]

The sentence does not explicitly state a preference for "becoming"; it poses an alternate "being" to another. But the negation of what "is," together with the futurial movement of "ought," clearly favors virtuality over actuality. It would seem that there are only two worlds between which Nin could move: some ideal world or (alas) some real world. But Nin's gesture is, after all, toward what "*ought* to be" and she seeks to make her ideal *the* real, a refuge from the "real" world on which the literal language of realism depended. "What ought to be" may be derived from the "dream," but its futurial direction signifies a flight away from any stable "real" already existing in the present. Nin yearned to transcend mundanity *and* the "in between" feeling; it sent her reeling out of both worlds. Nin implies that she could not linger for too long in *either* realm, and that she wouldn't privilege one over the other. In other words, though we know she was adamantly opposed to the kind of American realism she outlined in "Realism and Reality" (1946)[10] and *The Novel of the Future* (1968), she still valued the world realism represented. We all know the oft-quoted Jungian motto "Proceed from the dream outward" about which she cautioned people to avoid misinterpreting as a call to live as if in a *literal dream*.[11]

But without her foe, would she have been willing to abandon a representational model of literary philosophy? Toward the end of her life, Nin's writing was so well received that it accomplished both a legitimization of that heretofore misrepresented inner "dream" and, irrespective of the portion of reality that both camps may have shared, it affected linkages with scores of artists and fans, ultimately becoming a "journal of others."[12]

As I have said, Deleuzian thought is about becoming, not being. This distinction is related to the philosophical camps of idealism and empiricism, both of which conceive a "world" very differently. As Claire Colebrook explains in her study *Gilles Deleuze*:

> For an idealist, the only way in which we have a world or experience is if certain fundamental ideas can organize or constitute a world... We only have a *world* because what we receive...is mediated or organized by ideas. Idealism is, therefore, also a commitment to some notion of a subject who orders or constitutes their world *as a world*... Idealism acknowledges that there is a life and a real world outside our ideas, but it insists that this life...is *mediated* or conditioned by ideas... Deleuze argues against mediation[;]...life is lived directly and immediately... Empiricism, in contrast with idealism, argues that ideas do not order experience; ideas are the *effect* of experience.[13]

Literary realism, then, is suspect not because it purports to attempt to represent "reality," but because the attempt itself is premised on the notion that signs (words, in this case) mediate between "truth" and us. The "true world" takes on an almost divine reality, which results in a disease called "interpretosis," spread by interpreting "priests" that clog criticism with their pompous unveiling of "meaning" that supposedly exists behind those very signs.[14] As André Pierre Colombat explains, "the power of signs is based on an illusion, on a pious belief in the distinct order of the Signifier—the transcendental law, the Word of God, [etc.]."[15] Although Deleuze defined many different types of signs, signs should not impel us to ask what the "meaning" is behind them; rather "the 'sign' appears in the context of an encounter or an invention, in a space in between, not as a discovery" (Colombat 19). "This means," Colebrook would add, "that there is not a world (actual) that is *then* represented in images (virtual) by the privileged mind of man (the subject). Life is just this actual-virtual interaction of imaging: each flow of life becomes other in response to what is not" (Colebrook 87).[16]

As a point of clarification, note that in Deleuzian thought the binary is realism-versus-idealism, whereas in Nin's thought it is realism-versus-symbolism, surrealism, etc. But Deleuzian "realism" is the *opposite* of Nin's "realism." Both thinkers have different ways of conceiving the "enemy," so to speak, but Deleuze uses "realism" to mean something akin to what Nin means by "reality." Deleuze distrusts ideals that Platonic philosophers celebrate as *more real* than the mundane world of copies; Nin distrusts the mundane world itself, which realists pass off as "real." However, Nin does not point us to some better or more truthful world of essences, but to a new kind of *writing* about the world, just as Deleuze does. If Nin uses a dream-like system of signs, perhaps these signs are "diagrammatic or cartographic rather than symbolic or iconic."[17] Is it possible that Nin is in fact a writer who "de-territorializes" previous worlds and re-maps them at the instant of (re)creation?

In terms of novel-writing, Nin is sometimes charged with not giving her novels a narrative framework within which characters should move, interact, and respond. But this is precisely because she avoids positing an outside reality that characters then more or less approximate. Instead, her characters create worlds, as, for instance, with "stream of consciousness" passages. Colebrook explains that Deleuzian thought is likewise interested not in characters who respond to outside realities, but to the "flow of experience that runs through consciousness, producing and affecting characters, rather than being grounded in characters... [T]he 'narrative' often wander[s] undecidedly from one character's point of view to another" (Colebrook 84, 94).

Indeed, in much of Nin's writing, characters, whether in the *Diary* or from a novel, affect others through speech itself. In Deleuzian terms, this is "language itself as affect. This is where language is not meaning or message but closer to the dimension of noise, music, or sonorous style" (107), as for instance in Nin's famous birthing story in which the Anaïs-figure, as in a shamanic trance, repeatedly drums on her belly ("like a savage," the nurses exclaim). In this case, language drops off from representing some "truth" of history, the story, etc., and anaphorically functions *in and for itself*. It was very important for Nin to read this passage aloud at her lectures, for in doing so she was able to allow her speaking position as a woman to unfold rather than take for granted some pre-given speaking position which we would then demonstrate by example. If anything, Nin's characters often bleed together by way of this "dissolution" of subjectivity: it isn't always clear who is empathizing with whom or who "owns" the particular experience unfolding, stuttering.

I maintain that Anaïs Nin actualizes new worlds rather than properly representing them in reaction to realists. According to Andrew Gibson, this topic is of prime interest to feminism. In *Postmodernity, Ethics, and the Novel*, Gibson addresses something very similar to the tensions Krizan and Formentelli discuss. Following Nancy Harrison, Gibson uses a concept called "staging," which is particular to novels of "performance, a 'gestural presentation' of the lives of characters in which discourse is perceived as shaping those lives on the page."[18] The term emerges from a number of other concepts for which space cannot provide; suffice it to say, Gibson is concerned with feminism's friction with a "reality" that is "historically constructed by patriarchy" (Gibson 173). Following the work of Drucilla Cornell, Gibson finds women writers such as Jean Rhys and Anaïs Nin to be standing midway "between fiction and fact, representation and materiality, writing and the 'fundamental empirical reality of *actual* women.'"[19] "Ethical feminism," then, commits itself to a utopian ontology and epistemology; that is, what a woman can be occurs by way of "new metaphors" (174) and thus requires new representations. For Gibson, Nin writes with a tension between "actual experience" and "utopian possibility" (176). This isn't news to longtime Nin readers.

However, Gibson simply assigns the *Diary* to the "looking backward" documentary mode of narrative, while Nin's fiction is a mode "in which representation is powerfully transformed by the proleptic impulse" (176). The tension, he claims, is found in *Cities of the Interior*: it both asserts a "real" female experience and refutes classical mimesis. I suspect many readers would insist that Nin's *Diary* has a similar tension, not least because of *dédoublement*, but let us agree with Gibson that "Nin's narratives introduce a principle of irreducible self-difference which means that neither narrative present or narrative future is likely to be entirely comprehensible in terms of narrative past. So, too, with characterization: Nin's women are not altogether separate, 'fully individualized' figures. They are always becoming, do not petrify into being, exist primarily as sensibility[20] for that reason. The heroines thus continually cross boundaries and threaten to resemble each other more than they resemble themselves" (Gibson 180). Indeed, this "interchangeability of position" applies to the five books that make up the novel, Gibson points out, thus denying a "preordained and backward look" of "fixity" (180). It is interesting to note that the forward-looking Deleuze and Guattari encourage us to read each "plateau" or chapter of *A Thousand Plateaus* "independently of one another" (xx).

While I would disagree with the oversimplified method of Gibson's cleaving of *Diary* and novel, what he adds to the debate is a *temporal* understanding of the two binarized worlds of "reality." Nin's "proleptic impulse," her style of "utopian possibility" suggests, as does the title *The Novel of the Future*, that Nin was less interested in representing an alternative now to the realist *version* of now. I do not want to claim that this was Anaïs Nin's sole project, but I will suggest that the project comes, say, third in a series of stages. First she documents past events, which then blend into the translation of the "Dream" into real life, and finally she moves beyond the dream. The portion of Anaïs Nin's life after circa 1946 witnesses her building toward solutions to the real/dream dilemma. Inaugurating a world that "ought to be" required her to extend the problem from writing into reading and interpretation. The dream could be realized if we could only decipher the symbolic language that was so difficult to decipher. From astrology to psychoanalysis, Nin explored every system of interpretation available to her—classic Deleuzian experimentation. As John Rajchman points out, "Deleuze adopted the Proustian motto: the true dreamer is the one who goes out to verify something" (Rajchman 5).

One of the ways Nin helped bring the dream into the concrete outer world was to bring the symbols into the pre-written world, the world awaiting her literary representation. A project perhaps begun even before the "prime of life," she resolved to become an actress in those pre-written moments, to dramatize life even before she set her ink to paper. (Formentelli points to some of the personages from whom Nin probably took her cue: June Miller, Luise Rainer, and Maya Deren, for example.) This was quite a task, and it involved "act[ing upon] several stages at once...to be an 'actress' and, at the same time, a writer" (Formentelli 86). Nin did appear in some short films, but she envisioned dramatic playfulness and costume as necessary for bringing dream elements into the "everyday," even without the camera.

Returning home to write it all down Nin was nevertheless a reporter or journalist of a different stripe. "If the writing has a dream-like quality," Nin wrote, "it is not because the dramas I present are dreams, but because they are dramas as the unconscious lives them"; they "displace the over-obtrusive, dense, deceptive settings of our outer world which usually serve as a concealment" (*RR* 55). In her novels, a spade was never just a spade: every material object symbolized something. Moreover, she explained that her novels "contain both the symbol and the interpretation of the symbol" (*RR* 35), thus distancing herself from the dense allusions of other modernist writers. She hoped her referential objects pointed to something more "archetypal" perhaps, rather than literary or historical.

Nin simply attempted to construct a reality that her fellow or potential dreamers could access and recognize easily. I admit to possible objections that this project is, *on some level*, a case of interpretation rather than actualization. Abstraction from realist detail is "a process of distillation, of reduction to the barest essentials" (*RR* 35), she said, and required more work than that other brand of "reportage," which was only a mere transfer of "outer" world contents to paper. Such literature was not reality (*RR* 39), because its literal world had not yet been plied with the tools of "improvisation, free association, obedience to mood, impulse" and other such tools for finding the dream.[21] So equipped, she and her readers could abandon the need to hold dreams up to the world and measure the "accuracy" of their representation.

Another objection to my thesis might come by way of Nin's apparently idealistic love of "essence"—that which was left after removing the "dense, deceptive...concealment." Yet Nin strove only to simplify the complex web of the unconscious, to clear away the clutter she associated with American realism of her time, not just to explain away universal structures of the mind. It isn't as if her work exists in a vacuum, with no derivation from other realms. Rather, it functions less as a one-to-one *correspondence* or direct reference to a stable alternative world than it does as an *interface with* the alternative worlds derived from dreams, music, and architecture, all of which were *themselves* constructed from dreams and ideas that were not necessarily eternal or unchanging.

I reiterate that Anaïs Nin may have eventually wanted to forego a representational model altogether—even for the dream world. A representational model doesn't work for an ideal world because such a world would not yet exist, and it was a world that "ought to be" that interested her. Yet we needn't measure the correspondence between a world *here* and its literary representation *there*. Neither the "literal" nor the "figurative" need representation; indeed, representation appears as much more of a problem for truth-approximating realism in the first place. Nin's work thus enters a process of becoming, not so much being or even representing a world "out there" that would stand in oppositional status to literary artifice. As Nin explains, "My emphasis was on the *relation* between dream and reality, their *interdependence*" (*NF* 9, my emphasis). One was not the measure of the other, and she certainly did not advocate permanent rest in the dream: escape is not really possible for this woman who would then write that "the dream then, instead of being something apart from reality, a private world of fantasy and imagination, is actually an essential part of our reality..." (*NF* 23). It is no wonder readers rushed up to meet her *Diary*.

For Deleuze, good art *affects* a possible world. Not a world already existing and forever out of reach, but a world not yet *thought*, a world drawn from the "virtual" and made "actual"—not drawn from the actual and made representational. We should avoid becoming interpreting priests by obsessing with what symbols represent, with what is beyond the symbol. Such obsession, Deleuze and Guattari write, "is carried on into infinity and never encounters anything to interpret that is not already itself an interpretation" (*TP* 114). Thus, rather than seek the depth beyond the surface symbol, why not treat the symbol as an "image" itself, something legitimate and functional on its own? What we find in the secret depths are *themselves* representations of some idea anyway. We can abandon the surface/depth binary when we give up a search for an ultimate "real" world beneath the surface. I include Nin's dreamlike garden of real, too: if it was indeed produced by other images and ideas, there is no need for signs to operate as mere "symbols." Representation is tenuous: only some previous construction is being "represented." Language is already *as real* as the world; language *is* the world; language enacts becoming-worlds; language produces the world and not the reverse.

Good art draws from the virtual *new* ways of seeing the world. Nin's writing, then, can be seen not as drawing from an *actual* or "real" world of dreams in opposition to the real*ism* world of *non*representational objects—quite the reverse. Nin's striving for what "ought" to be places her, in my view, in line with those writers who draw from virtual possibilities and then actualize them. Indeed, "if [perceptions] resemble something [that already exists 'out there'], it is with a resemblance produced with their own methods; and the smile on the canvas is made solely with colors, lines, shadow, and light. If resemblance haunts the work of art, it is because sensation refers only to its material."[22]

Even after all this, Nin remains an autobiographer, a diarist, a backwards-looking writer. But we know all too well the chasm between what she wrote and what "really happened," at least according to historians and biographers. I can only insist that Nin's work legitimates itself by creating images not reducible to representations so that the becoming-dream might even enact a forgetting. ◈

Notes

[1] Smith, Daniel W. "'A Life of Pure Immanence': Deleuze's 'Critique et Clinique' Project." Introduction to *Essays Critical and Clinical*. Minneapolis: University of Minnesota Press, 1997. xi-lvi.

[2] Artaud, Antonin. "Here Lies." In *Selected Writings*, ed. Susan Sontag, trans. Helen Weaver. New York: Farrar Straus & Giroux, 1977. 540. Cited in Smith. 180.

[3] Deleuze, Gilles, and Félix Guattari. *A Thousand Plateaus: Capitalism and Schizophrenia*, trans. Brian Massumi. Minneapolis: University of Minnesota Press, 1987. Given in the text as *TP*. See especially pp. 149-166.

[4] See also Deleuze, Gilles, and Félix Guattari. *Kafka: Towards a Minor Literature*, trans. D. Polan. Minneapolis: University of Minnesota Press, 1986.

[5] Deleuze. *Difference and Repetition*. New York: Columbia University Press, 1994. 212.

[6] Nin, Anaïs. *The Novel of the Future*. Athens: Swallow press/Ohio University Press, 1968. 24. Given in the text as *NF*. Evelyn J. Hinz's *The Mirror and the Garden: Realism and Reality in the Writings of Anaïs Nin* (New York: Harcourt brace Jovanovich, 1971), is still the best work on Nin's privileging of "garden" writing over "mirror" (realist) writing.

[7] Krizan, Kim. "Illusion and the Art of Survival: Tracing the Origins of Nin's Creativity." *ANAIS: An International Journal*, vol. 10, 1992. 18.

[8] Formentelli, Beatrice. "The Difficulty of the Real: A French Perspective." *ANAIS: An International Journal*, vol. 2, 1984. 77.

[9] Nin. *The Diary of Anaïs Nin. Vol. 4, 1944-1947*. Ed. Gunther Stuhlmann. New York: Harcourt Brace, 1971. 177.

[10] "Realism and Reality—A Pamphlet." Reproduced in *ANAIS: An International Journal*, vol. 8, 1990. Given in the text as *RR*.

[11] See, for instance, her conversation with Henry Miller in the film *Anaïs Nin Observed*. Robert Snyder, dir. Mystic Fire Video, 1995.

[12] The one who should be credited as the first to theorize Nin and Deleuze together is Mai Al-Nakib, who writes of the rhizomatic, ever-reaching and link-

seeking quality of the *Diary*, one that "is a secret which contains its own discovery within it rather than in opposition to it." See "Anaïs Nin's *Diary* as Deleuzian Rhizome" in *ANAIS: An International Journal*, vol. 17, 1999. 79.

[13] Colebrook, Claire. *Gilles Deleuze*. New York and London: Routledge, 2000. 79-80.

[14] Deleuze and Guattari. *A Thousand Plateaus: Capitalism and Schizophrenia*. 114.

[15] Colombat, André Pierre. "Deleuze and Signs." In *Deleuze and Literature*. Ian Buchanan and John Marks, eds. Edinburgh University Press, 2000. 15.

[16] One should be careful, Colebrook warns, not to place the virtual on the side of the "unreal" copy, transcript, or representation of that which becomes real and actual: the virtual is far more than a copy; its pure potential to become something actual (99). Besides, this is not a Baudrillardian world in which signs no longer refer to an external reality but instead to other signs; this is a world where signs bring the virtual into the actual. If they bear resemblance to an external reality, it is only because they are simulacrum, copies for which there are no originals.

[17] Rajchma, John. *The Deleuze Connections*. Cambridge and London: MIT Press, 2000. 67.

[18] Gibson, Andrew. *Postmodernity, Ethics, and the Novel: From Leavis to Levinas*. New York: Routledge, 1999. 170.

[19] Gibson (173) quotes Cornell from *Beyond Accommodation: Ethical Feminism, Deconstruction, and the Law*. London: Routledge, 1991. 3.

[20] Gibson goes on to discuss Nin as a writer of "sensibility" rather than of "cognition"; that is, Nin writes with an "openness" to an idea or object that cognition would only seek to "master" (162). Interestingly, "sensibility" here appears very much akin to Keats' "negative capability."

[21] "On Writing" (1947) is also reproduced in *ANAIS: An International Journal*, vol. 8, 1990.

[22] Deleuze and Guattari. *What is Philosophy?* New York: Columbia University Press, 1994. 166.

Karin Finell

Anaïs Remembered
February 22, 1977

Your day, yesterday, it rained.
A tender kind of rain.
Had you been placed within the earth
the sky would desire to caress you.
Had you been placed within a grave
I'd bring you flowers, still
proteas, cymbidium, exotic blossoms.
But now the sea holds you
after the purifying flame, Fire—
then water.
Anaïs—my fingers write your name upon the sand.
Mermaid-woman,
You influenced many.
Awakened dreams,
Taught us to be ourselves.
Mother and Muse
Source and Sorceress.
Returned now to your undersea-world of coral and amber,
Swimming with sea-weed in your hair
Your eyes ever changing from gray-green
to turquoise to topaz-gold.
And as this day is dying,
The sky is painted with your palette.
The hot orange sun
as if abandoned in embrace
falls to the sea
Fire to water.
The sea a quiet mirror now,
from which,
as out of Neptune's shell,
You will arise again.

Thomas March

Keeping the Diary
The art of reflection in a solipsistic age

I began my Diary, on Monday, June 22, 1992. I was nineteen years old. Both Anaïs Nin and Henry Miller made appearances in the first paragraph, in which I sought to situate myself in a tradition of diary writers by arguing against Miller's criticisms of the diary writing enterprise. But I could just as easily have begun with his praises. My attitude toward my own diary has come to resemble, more and more, Miller's ambivalence. Too many times I have gone back to an earlier volume of my diary, to remember a date or a place or whether I had always felt a particular way about a thing, only to find myself cringing at my early blindness to the world around me, my apparent belief that it was enough simply to record my reactions to the world, without providing much sense of where those reactions came from or what they might lead to. I like to think that this has improved with time, and whatever familiarity with the operations of Life that time brings, but it is a constant struggle for anyone who wants to write a diary that is more than just a release valve that thoroughly exhausts its value in the moment of composition.

The second paragraph of my first entry contains just the kind of embarrassing exuberance and self-aggrandizement that diaries too often harbor—and that make people wary of the diary as a literary form. It begins: "I am compelled to begin this exercise in self-infatuation more to rescue myself than to congratulate myself." This could have told me more about my "self-infatuation" had I bothered to examine the significance of the notions of rescue and congratulation that I only begin to invoke here. Instead, I move on to various teenaged ruminations on writing and sensuality, of which I had, at that time, experienced almost none except what I found on others' pages and mechanically tried to reproduce in my own experience, mistaking the movements for the methods themselves. Although my choice of words tended toward the grandiose—I was "rescuing" myself, after all—at least I recognized that there was some redemptive potential in diary writing. Maybe I thought I was rescuing myself from indolence by imposing daily writing practice. I like to think that, by beginning a discipline of reflection, however feeble, I was rescuing myself from the effects of the very blinding self-infatuation that, even in this brief passage, I identify as an essential quality of the diary. I want to believe that I had that kind of insight. But I didn't leave myself much evidence to confirm or deny this. It's all bold pronouncements and emotional schemes, with too little of the reflection on origins and implications of emotions that would render it a document of Life, rather than just a display case in which a few of Life's facts have been thoughtlessly arranged.

Since that first entry my diary has served a number of purposes. I've used it simply as a place to record the facts of events or the products of unreflective, ranting moments of emotional exuberance. But in my better moments, and as the diary evolved alongside my understanding of its potential, it became a place where diagnosis of the world and myself yielded to more productive analysis of each. That is, I became less satisfied with the simple act of reportage and began to take advantage of the diary's potential as a place in which to organize and make sense of experience, and thus to reveal the creative nature of our arrangements of experience, of life itself.

It's not especially groundbreaking, this suggestion that diaries help us to explore the significance of experience, but it's very easy for a diary to miss this mark. Typical objections to the diary as a literary form—that it is too fantastical, all whimsy and solipsism, a dull and self-absorbed catalog of events in shorthand that make up only the most banal touchstones of a life—are not entirely unfounded. Some accuse diaries of functioning as distractions from life, from full experience. Only the solipsistic diary cannot answer these charges. The solipsist endows each experience with a significance that arises only from the fact that it has happened to *him*. He is interested only in the existence of his impressions of the world and does not test them or seek to understand them. He gives them only expression, with no sense that a dialogue has just begun, one in which he refuses to participate.

The reflective diary, on the other hand, promises more than a history of private enthusiasms or grievances. Beyond titillation, beyond our voyeuristic impulses (of which Nin was masterfully aware), we come to a diary on a search for insight into a particular life and, when we find it, into the patterns and penchants of our own lives. For readers and writers, it is the same. The diary may begin with a visceral appeal to our need for a repository of secrets or silliness, or as a tool for spiritual dialysis—the cleansing power of confession for the writer, and for the reader the cathartic or reinforcing power of having received such a confession. Even more appealing might be the thrill and comfort a diary provides by lending in its relative permanence an air of importance that can transcend the words themselves. But whether writing in a diary, reading our own diaries, or reading the diaries of others, we have an opportunity to come into contact with greater awareness of what comprises the process of living. When we fail to reflect like this in our own lives, to discover our own secrets or at least gesture toward their discovery by asking and seeking to answer questions about significance, reading a reflective diary can remind us that this is what we do and how, that we are interesting subjects of inspection in our own right. Introspection represents a step in the right direction, as it allows us, at the very least, to give a name to what's happening in our heads. But beyond that, either we decide to be content simply with regurgitating what we've found there or we examine where it came from, what it's doing, and where it might go.

The reflective diary reveals how each day, or each moment stolen to reflect upon each day, each week, each month, is full of significance. The reflective diary is at the very least an attempt to answer the questions, "How do I live, and what does it mean that I do it this way?" Not everyone asks, and those who do don't ask all the time. Diary writers are reflective in proportion to the degree to which they seek to articulate the full dimensions of their experience—not only the facts of and emotions that make up everyday life, but their external stimuli and internal motivations. The closer a diarist gets to the fullness of this articulation, the greater everyone's insight into how experience and its meanings come to be. The analysis may not be correct or complete, but it will be the way toward whatever understanding we are capable of having in the moment of writing or reading. There may be opportunities for amendment later. But if we aren't in the habit of reflecting in the first place, it is less likely that we will ever take the time to ask whether we were wrong, whether and why envy or jealousy once led us to dislike someone for whom we now might have the most affection. We can only ask the question, knowing that it is an endless one and that it makes no sense, yields no answer, unless we ask it from as many angles as possible.

Each moment of focused reflection that a diary affords can become a reminder that we do more when we live than just move, eat, feel, breathe and begin again. Life degenerates too easily into reflex—loving and hating just as easily as having the same thing for dinner every Tuesday night. Over a century of psychoanalysis has reminded us that we experience the events and emotions of life according to interpretive structures designed to connect us to the reality of the external world while simultaneously preparing us to receive that world in terms that are amenable to our own most cherished myths of what that reality should be. We do not simply receive a world, or on the other hand flex ourselves against it, but are in the struggle between reception and projective flexing, bringing all that we have known, seen, or believed to bear upon making sense of the moment that presents itself. Some moments seem simpler. We put on the left shoe first. But even these can be endowed with meaning, can hold some clue as to how we are in the world. Father used to put his left shoe on first; or maybe it was his right, and there is rebellion in the simple act of dressing against an old and arbitrary order your father insisted upon. When it reflects upon Life most fully, the diary reminds us that we are not passive, but constantly reading, interacting, and creating, projecting our fears and hopes onto the cleanly swept sidewalks of one street, onto the first bundle of a particular spring flower in the corner bodega, conjuring all there is of spring and the best and worst events of a lifetime of Aprils and Mays.

The reflective diary can facilitate a greater awareness of how this happens. By reflecting as well as recording, questioning as well as answering, explaining alongside judging, it lays bare the process according to which experience of the moment, of the day, of the world, has come into being. However it might manifest itself in the particulars of any individual case, the reflective diary uncovers the process of struggling against, and often succumbing to, our assumptions about how the world must operate, of noticing our reactions to experience and tracking down their origins as well as we can. Ultimately, the reasons for keeping or reading a diary are relatively unimportant—as personal history, as an artist's distillery of ideas, even as a means by which to exorcise darker and coarser tempers—because each purpose will be served if the diary is in the first place reflective. When we see experience thus reflected and reflected upon in the diary, in our own or in someone else's attempts, when we see Life emerge in continuous and converging streams of relation and significance, we can begin not only to understand ourselves better but to understand others better by acknowledging their equal claim to the fullness of experience that we claim for ourselves.

This is not to say that writing or reading a diary with understanding in mind necessarily results in the achievement of a final awareness or truth. There will always be newer truths that force us to amend or reevaluate our current truths, and as these become revealed as comfortable, practical conveniences, we understand better where we were and what had to be surmounted in order for us to become as we are. In my own first diary entry, I find my earlier self reaching to articulate a rationale for writing, in words he only barely understood. I know better now why I write, in the diary or anywhere else, but I forgive the bold confusion of that early entry for what it gives me now. The obnoxious melodrama of a decade ago has yielded, at least in part, to an enlarged appreciation for what the diary can do. In the difference between the two, I believe that the future may hold more of the same— that I might continue to better understand my own life, and Life itself, and if that's the best I can do, it's still better than the alternative.

One of the most renowned diarists of the last century, Anaïs Nin devoted her creative life to the exploration of this kind of understanding. Not accidentally, she also possessed an awareness of the value of the diary-writing process itself. In *The Novel of the Future*, her letters, and in the *Diary*, Nin reveals her appreciation of diary writing as an art, and consequently, as a revelation of the art of life itself. In her essay "The New Woman," Nin writes that "[w]e write to taste life twice, in the moment and in retrospection" (*Mystic of Sex*, 96). Nin is, above all else, an advocate of life, of writing as a celebration of life— not in the purely hedonistic manner that has come to be associated with her name in some circles, but in a respectful, sympathetic and compassionate manner that broadly embraces the Thoreauvian desperation of a multitude of otherwise unknowable characters, as well as the frenzied and ersatz connections of human revelry. It is there in the *Diary*, and in the fiction, best realized in *A Spy in the House of Love*, *Seduction of the Minotaur* and *Collages*. These all share a principle of revealing life as it comes to be made by those living it.

It is the unabashedly contingent quality of this knowing that makes the diary suspect, to some. Aside from accusations and temptations of solipsism, the difficulty of the diary as a literary form—a difficulty it shares with the memoir—lies in its implicit and simultaneous claims to historical truth and the aesthetic exigencies of fictional narrative. A common complaint among detractors, Nin's especially, is that diaries are too tolerant of lies and misrepresentations, that they are unreliable. Of course, people don't like to have their names in someone else's diary, associated with actions in which they never engaged or words they never said. It may seem at best impolite or sloppy, at worst malevolent. Even a diary that purports to be a record of historical fact is the product of an individual consciousness, engaged in a daily recording of events and their significance that necessarily restricts the wisdom of its historical understanding to a present moment in which the significance of events has yet to emerge fully. A diary is first and foremost a personal document; diarists can speak with authority only about their own experiences, and their gestures toward understanding others' points of view are necessarily framed by the kinds of unavoidable idiosyncrasies of exaggeration and omission that a historian would at least attempt to overcome. Embellishment is only a flaw according to the historian's criteria of truth and accuracy, of attributing acts and utterances to the appropriate agents, or, at the very least, to continue to suggest that such certainty is always available and not merely a goal toward which the historian asymptotically creeps.

But when our appreciation of a diary's truth remains exclusively historical or "factual," we overlook what the diary can tell us about truth telling itself. We don't expect or enjoy outright lies. But what constitutes such a lie—placing the emphasis differently than others who claim the same experience? Or is it putting words in people's mouths, words they never said but may be imagined to have said? Or, worse yet perhaps, is it testimony to the occurrence of events that never happened—not just endowing events with an objectionable order or significance but claiming that the car door slammed when it was never open in the first place, or that the lively dinner party was in fact a night home alone? We may be right to object when such distortions obscure the truth we seek from the reading of a diary. But we would do well to remember that the most strenuous accusations may have their source in the revelation of an uncomfortable truth, something new we had failed to consider or something old we had once suspected but had otherwise successfully repressed. We would do even better to accept, even in the face of pure fabrication, that what we can call a lie with satisfaction and conviction can still tell us something about the liar.

It may seem ironic that the enhancement of understanding was Anaïs Nin's goal when she edited her *Diary* for publication. We know that, in fact, she excised enormous amounts of material in order to avoid revealing the breadth and depth of her love affairs. But full disclosure was not the principle of truth that guided Nin's efforts. In *The Novel of the Future*, she asserts that her goal in editing the *Diary* was to achieve a more comprehensive representation of the truth. "The solution to the danger of truth," she writes, "lies in making a portrait so full and rich that all sides are heard, all aspects considered" (152). The result of adhering to such a principle would be the representation not of a single truth, but of a constellation of receptions of the world masquerading, in the consciousness of each individual, as a "truth" that functions as the equivalent of reality. This sensitivity to the conditional or personal quality of "truth" reveals once again the influence of a Freudian metapsychology, filtered here through the lens of Otto Rank, that Nin so often sought, consciously or not, to fictionalize. When she suggests that the fullest representation of a situation's truth requires that "all sides" and "all aspects" be taken into account, Nin is doing more than garnishing the timeworn wisdom that different people see things differently. Rather, she is urging us, as R.D. Laing* does, to

---

*R.D. Laing was a controversial existentialist psychologist and philosopher who believed contemporary society attempts to rob one of individuality. His The Divided Self (1960) is considered a seminal work regarding the experiences of the mentally ill. While lambasted by conventional practitioners, his work was praised by patients, who claimed Laing knew how they truly felt.—Ed.

recognize this difference as the source of our most deeply entrenched conflicts, our inability to understand one another completely.

Like Laing, Nin seems to acknowledge the intractability of such difference and disconnection while maintaining a curious faith in the ability of human beings to achieve moments of connection, if only by means of mystical intervention. For Nin, the *Diary*, the process of *editing* it, creates a space in which she may at least gesture toward this possibility. In *Aspects of the Novel*, E.M. Forster writes:

> We cannot understand each other, except in a rough and ready way; we cannot reveal ourselves, even when we want to; what we call intimacy is only makeshift; perfect knowledge is an illusion. But in the novel we can know people perfectly, and...we can find here a compensation for their dimness in life (63).

In her fiction Nin attempts, by revealing the interior lives of her characters, to compensate for their "dimness" in the life that happens outside of fiction, when we can see them only from the outside. She similarly envisions the *Diary* as a great laboratory of understanding, a place where she can compensate for this dimness by doing all she can to uncover and elucidate the motivations and private dramas of those who enter her life. By returning to edit the *Diary*, Nin is attempting to reinforce its potential as an example, by virtue of its chronological scope as well as of the reflective quality of its individual entries, in the degree to which the struggle for understanding of others, as well as of the self, shapes her representations of experience. Nin writes, again in *The Novel of the Future*, that "[t]he destructive aspect of truth is neutralized by a deep probing into motivation which makes one understand a character, and what is understood is not condemned" (151). She thus brings to her representation of her own life the same sensitivity to her characters' interiority that lies at the foundation of her fiction, and the figures of her life are revealed as characters in their own right. This desire to understand others, and by extension to understand one's place in relation to them, is an appeal for us to appreciate a particular *ethos* of the diarist. By embracing this quality of the diarist's consciousness, the *Diary* then comes to stand also as a recognition of the other as a creating, and not only created, entity, whose truth is only partially available in the version of it perceived by the diarist. That is, others may exist largely as products of the diarist's fantasy or fancy, but they receive the benefit of a respect that acknowledges the legitimacy of their own private experience, even if it might ultimately remain inaccessible or misinterpreted.

Does editing, even for enhanced understanding, destroy the conceit of spontaneity that makes up so much of a diary's appeal? We come to a diary seeking to understand what a life was like from day to day, how a particular individual made sense of his or her experience of the world, without the benefit of hindsight or any knowledge more perfect than the apparent significance of the anxieties, joys, compulsions, and blindness of that particular moment. Nin valued her diary precisely for the spontaneity it allowed: "I enjoyed writing the diary more than I did the novels because it was unplanned, spontaneous" (162). This is not to say, however, that such spontaneity is antithetical to reflection, merely that the motivation for diaristic reflection stems primarily from an urge to record and understand that is not concerned with any organization beyond that required for its fullest, most immediate expression. Nin contrasts this spontaneity to the ostensibly more organized work of writing fiction: "In the novels, I am aware of being a craftsman. Not in the diary" (162). A novel may require more sustained consciousness of craft, but craft itself is never far from the consciousness of anyone who writes regularly. Concerns of craft do not necessarily evaporate but yield to the urgency of expression or to the need for unfettered exploration of the significance of what one has just experienced. And in the kind of editing Nin proposes, the early products of spontaneity are not necessarily erased but improved upon, treated in some cases as a sketch or an outline ready to receive more subtle shadings of understanding that bring it more fully to life.

Nin claims of her editing work that she has only engaged in refinement: "I have not changed anything in the diary, only omitted what was unimportant, trivial, or repetitious" (153). The publication of the unexpurgated *Diary* has shown that this is certainly an understatement. Any contrasts between the unexpurgated work and the versions edited by Nin underscore the fact that Nin's editing was not just an attempt to refine but was in fact an act of framing and re-framing the truth. Does the edited *Diary*, then, in its coming into being as the result of present motivations foisted upon the representation of the past, become memoir instead, a diary only in that its reflections have (supposed) dates of composition attached? A diarist can always return to edit earlier portions the diary for the purpose of ensuring accuracy, with the almost irresistible, mostly unconscious urge to endow earlier entries with a prescient quality that comes from the introduction of present understanding of the significance of past events into the narrated life of a particular time. A diary tells our stories, to ourselves and to others, more completely than a memoir ever could. A memoir must work with whatever material remains in memory, and the repressions, elisions, and erasures engendered by the demands of the present. The best memoirs cannot seek to represent the nuances in the development of an entire life but, rather, give us exemplary moments. The diary, on the other hand, treats each moment as exemplary. We can only condemn bad editing, the kind that refuses to bring these moments more completely to life, or limits understanding by stunting it rather than enriching it.

This principle of editing for enhanced or enriched understanding should inform every return to a diary, whether our own or someone else's. We don't need to have pens in our hands. We need only our knowledge of how things have turned out and to let that stand against our earlier attempts at understanding and reveal in the difference the ignorance, however subtle, of our past positions. Again and again we find our interpretive temperaments informed by a perverse and private blindness that had masqueraded as clarity. It's inevitable, and it's humiliating, in the most enervating sense of the word, to discover ourselves as incomplete, however strenuously we may have exerted ourselves in a quest to be thorough, to explore every possibility of cause and effect that brought us to the emotion or the impression that produced sufficient motivation for recording it. Discovering the difference between memory and what we attested to in the past, and finding ourselves unbelievable even in black and white, are overwhelming reminders that the process of coming to understanding or, rather, of articulating the most *complete* understanding, however short it must ultimately fall, is the work of a lifetime. This editing, too, is continuous; today's insight into the omissions of the past will be revealed next week as another bout of blindness, now of a different sort. We bring that understanding to our present pages, to warn away any sense of the infallibility of our impressions of the world and those in it.

If you know who you are, what peculiar propensities for inventing and reinventing you are likely to indulge, the misapprehensions or gaps in understanding that you find in past entries may come as less of a surprise. Nevertheless, rereading may entertain you, or it may stop your heart at the return of an anxiously or even indifferently repressed awareness that some event, some character was more or less important than originally cast. If the diary has been as comprehensively reflective as you could make it, you will have provided yourself at least with an outline of how you have changed. Returning can be catastrophic or comforting, enraging or amusing, and sometimes all of these things at once, but this is far better than having your heart stop from emptiness, from having nothing to return to but pages black with an abundance of narcissistic ranting.

Some have suggested that, rather than encouraging narcissistic excesses of experience, elevating the diary only tempts people to retreat from life. Why is there so much fear about what the diary replaces or distracts from? Is it because there may never be anything to show for it? Because it may tell uncomfortable truths that privacy protects from cross-examination? The achievement of balance, of recognizing the value of competing demands on one's time and energy, is never an easy task. Poets who are diarists, bankers who are diarists, and diarists with demanding lovers are all faced with difficult choices. But what better place to achieve that balance than in the opportunity that the diary provides, as a space devoted to reflection in the moment and, in the success of that work, to the provocation or renewed reflection upon return?

The intensity of this reflection, especially when concentrated in the habitual act of keeping a diary, may seem to be a distraction from the very process of living richly that it seeks to support. Even if we acknowledge the diary as an enriching form of art in its own right, there is still the matter to consider of its "deleterious effect" upon the pursuit of other art. During the months of October and November 1933, Nin herself had to parry arguments from Henry Miller and Otto Rank against the value of the diary. Miller suggests that the diary is a distraction from other artistic pursuits and that it encourages artistic shorthand incapable of supporting the nuance required to maintain a robust fictional universe. In Rank's estimation, the diary interferes with the psychoanalytic process and, by implication, any sustained striving toward self-awareness. In spite of their differences in orientation, these arguments share a concern that the diary, instead of facilitating the development of understanding, actually impedes it in a number of ways.

In a letter to Nin dated October 12, 1933, Miller characterizes Nin's diary as an impediment to her development as a writer: "The hours that go to the journal are an evasion, fundamentally, of the imminent, the ever-impending problem—that of mastering your medium, of becoming the artist you are" (*A Literate Passion*, 217-218). In the same letter, Miller blames the diary for the fact that Nin's fiction of this period is so often, in his opinion, "all shrieks, all abstracts" (218). Miller blames Nin's engagement with the diary for what he characterizes as her inability to confront the challenges of pacing and structure in her other fictional work. He writes that "perhaps this is one of the great failings of writing a diary instantly after a thing happens— it frustrates the needed accumulation of drag and slag, of flesh and blood, of obscurities and obstacles and obfuscations, which because they must be tackled and offer one resistance produce inevitably the quality of art" (218). This may seem a fair assessment, as Nin herself later suggested that she appreciated that the composition of the diary allowed her to forego consciousness of craft in favor of spontaneity. But Miller associates diary writing in general with the production of unreflective prose that, as it cuts corners in the service of immediate expression, inevitably avoids confrontation with the infrastructure of experience. He elaborates on this idea by further suggesting that the process of diary writing, not just in the example of Nin's diary, is merely and at best a rehearsal for the more important work of fictional composition:

> Avoid grappling with these and you have a surface affair—a linear pattern, a solo melody in one key and monotonous and eventually exasperating. I ask myself, isn't it this precisely which gives a diary its essential character? Is it not like the sketch which an artist employs for the final architecture? Is it not the thin melody on which the composer sets to work, and from this slender, given clue, spins his luxurious, compact web? You see, I am aiming seriously at the destruction of this diary (218-219).

Whether as a "sketch" or a "thin melody," a diary has no value in and of itself, in Miller's estimation. The best it can aspire to be is a warehouse for the raw material that will someday become useful in the shaping of more "luxurious," and thus more important, work.

Even if this were a characteristic failure of Nin's diary of this time, such shortsightedness is not a necessary failure of the diary as a form of writerly enterprise. If there is ever a histrionic quality to Nin's style, a lack of subtlety, as Miller accuses here, it is not the diary's fault. Nin does learn to "grapple" with the questions required of one who would explore understanding, make understanding possible. And she does it in her diary. Nor does the diary, as Miller would have it and as Nin implies in her ostensible rejection of craft as a major concern for the diarist, always impede the development of formal skill or a reflective orientation. In his introduction to *A Literate Passion*, Gunther Stuhlmann refers to Nin's diary as "her refuge, her workshop, and the act of writing her only stabilizer" (vii). It is a workshop that does not delay or distract from an engagement with life but records that engagement and in doing so deepens and propels it, time after time. Nin's diary did function as a workshop, in that her self-examination and attempts there to understand the motivations and private realities of others—however correct or incorrect they themselves might have found them—fostered Nin's creation of sympathetic portraits of characters in her fiction. It allowed her to refine her ability to describe experience as fully as possible, moving beyond mere observations of dull facts (whether of events or emotions) toward the articulation of their effects and explanation of their causes.

Miller seems to have recognized that Nin's diary is more than a blueprint when he writes, in a letter dated October 17, 1933, that it "is a great human document, with all its faults, and perhaps just because of its faults, because they are as revelatory of your personality as the perfections!" (223) However, in spite of this apparent recognition of the diary as a repository of experience whose value lies in the access it provides to the machinations of the human mind, he is at best ambivalent, as he continues to urge Nin "to drop [her] god-damned diary someday" (223). Miller's complaint against perceived deficiencies in Nin's style is in fact an argument against the kinds of deficiencies that arise from failing to go beyond responses to things in order to investigate their causes—and consequently failing to recognize in others the very same complexity of experience. These are the very deficiencies that Nin later seeks to correct by adopting the ethos of "understanding."

Whatever her motivations, and whatever their truth, Nin's entries concerning Otto Rank's idea of sacrificing the diary establish the dimensions of an alternate argument to Miller's, one that also condemns it as an evasion and distraction from more important work. In *Incest*, Nin claims relief at having abandoned the diary, in compliance with Rank's wishes:

> On November 8, 1933, Rank asked me to give up my journal and I left it in his hands. He delivered me of my opium.
> It was a bold stroke. It stunned me. It was a violation (294).

It may seem surprising that Nin complies with this request. Then again, this entry itself proves that she has not completely abandoned the enterprise. She quotes Rank as having said to her that the diary is her "last defense against analysis" (294). Rank is certainly correct when he suggests that, unlike the analytical process, diary writing, no matter how reflective, cannot entirely replicate the analyst's sometime role as an editor in his own right, identifying the presence of omissions and gaps in the story that would otherwise go unnoticed and unexplored, burying any chance at insight into their significance to the story itself.

But Nin's response to this notion is to articulate the principles of a more perfect diary, one in which the urge toward evasion is minimized. She credits Rank for his insight into the diary's appeal as a tool for evasion, but as an insight that includes an appreciation for its ability to facilitate the creation of a space in which a great deal of reflective work can be accomplished:

> He has understood so quickly the role of refuge played by the diary, the role of a personage with whom a dialogue could help me resist invasion of the self. He has understood what a shell the diary is around me, what a weapon of defense. But he has understood, too, that it contains the *truth*, and that this truth, which I feel compelled to tell somewhere, I can tell him, since I have written it in that diary he kept. I talked to Rank as I talk to my journal (297).

Here, Nin is rejecting the idea that it is within the nature of the diary writing enterprise to facilitate self-deception and the avoidance of critical, reflective engagements. She equates writing in the diary with talking to Rank. And while this assertion of equivalence necessarily ignores important differences between the qualities of dialogue one can have with oneself as opposed to with an external listener, it implies Nin's rejection of the idea of a diary that serves *only* as a "refuge" or defense against "invasion." In other words, by acquiescing to Rank (at least in theory), Nin is, ironically, attempting to reaffirm her diary's central role in the pursuit of self-knowledge.

Any diary demands its dues. But to what extent does it dissipate or greedily absorb the creative or reflective impulse, whether it would be otherwise expressed in psychoanalysis, in a sonnet, in a conversation with a friend over a cup of coffee, or in a long walk? A diary can require that other things—relationships, other art—be neglected in the service of its demands, but that is the danger of any form of reflective work. Perhaps it is too much to ask, for a commitment to the art of the diary as well as the art of the novel or the poem, or even a full social calendar and a life in which no relationship ever goes without nurturing, even for a day. But to suggest that the diary must be abandoned for the sake of other reflective work is to suggest that neither can be informed or enhanced by the other. To abandon the pursuit of one or the other, to submit to the idea that you must be one thing *or* another, is to replace the potential for awareness with a simple removal of tension. The extent of the absorption depends upon the particular needs of the diarist. The choice of one thing over another is a choice *in time* that does not negate other pursuits or even fully distract from them. The struggle with the material of experience isn't *over* when it finds its way into the diary. Reflection is an ever-renewing resource.

Nin's pretense of giving up her diary doesn't last long, and it doesn't need to, as she articulates an understanding of its function that refutes the charge of evasion. On February 6, 1934, Nin writes in *Diary 2*, referring back to the episode with Rank, that she began a new "notebook" to replace the diary she has abandoned to Rank:

> A month or so later I began the portrait of Rank in a diary volume, and Rank did not feel it was the diary I had resuscitated but a notebook, perhaps. The difference is subtle and difficult to seize. But I sense it. It consists chiefly of *not nurturing the neurotic plant* (306).

This is not a denial of the diary's appeal as an accomplice in evasion but an assertion that this appeal can be minimized and overcome. The distinction Nin draws between a "diary" and a "notebook" is provisional and serves chiefly to mark a rejection of the diary's purely escapist temptations in favor of a more reflective approach. The difference between the "notebook" and the "diary" consists not of any decrease in intensity or devotion of time and energy, but in the purpose toward which these energies will be directed. That is, the ever-present neurotic plant, if it cannot die, will at least receive no more sustenance in the pages of the diary. Nin is not attempting to deny the existence of or to eradicate the neurotic plant, or even its influence upon the motivations for how and what one writes. Escape and lack of confrontation nurture neurosis; exposure to reflection and analysis begins to cut off the nutrients of repression and indolence on which it feeds. It is solipsistic diary writing—that is, using the diary only to express the symptoms of neurosis, or the mere facts of experience, without concern for their origins and the new knowledge and perspectives that an attempt to identify these origins might provide—that "nurtures" such neurotic stasis. Whether by refusing to nurture the "neurotic plant" Nin was really effecting a stylistic change is not as important as the fact that this transition represents a burgeoning awareness of solipsism's dangerous denial of the complexity and nuance of life.

The diary is not always an antidote to solipsism but always represents the promise of a reflective space that can reveal solipsism for what it is, a degradation of Life. Both Miller and Rank correctly identify the diary's unique capacity for sustaining unreflective work; and even if this is not an essential quality of the diary as an enterprise, its pretense of privacy can encourage self-expression in which the mechanisms of experience are ignored. When the diary is only a refuge, it is a hothouse for the "neurotic plant" that steals the nourishment away from and stunts the growth of reflective inquiry and awareness by devoting resources instead to the simple reinforcement of the sufficiency of first impressions. In spite of its pretense of celebrating the self, the solipsistic diarist thus cheapens life, in his failure to consider the interactive, creative nature of experience. His is a record of caricatures rather than characters, of cartoonish figures who function only as repositories of emotions and reactions whose universe of possible sources remains unexplored. We can come to only the roughest understanding of that particular consciousness, which has given us only enough information to reduce it to a type. Even solipsistic lapses are redeemable if quickly followed by a corresponding digestion while the circumstances are still fresh—a revisitation like Nin's edits for understanding—or the significance of the experience that produced the emotion is forever shut away. In the retrospection that emerges from our own later reading, or from the readings of others, it may become clear whether the representation of a particular day has been motivated by the grandiosity of some irresistible pathology or simply by the equally compelling need to get by, to elide here and exaggerate there in order to maintain the careful and unconscious illusions of our daily realities of self and others. But the solipsistic diary sets the self apart in secrecy and knows only the histrionic and anxious language of self-validation, alienating anyone who may come to it, even the writer's subsequent selves, in search for a model of understanding. The solipsist retreats from Life—and when the diary functions only as a refuge, as a turning away from life, it will always be incomplete.

A diary may not convince anyone of what constitutes a proper life, but it might provide the kind of blood transfusion that Nin claims Miller's *Tropic of Cancer* to be. Then again, it is more like a surgery, a peeling back of the surface of life to reveal what constitutes it in the first place. The reflective diary is a faithful reminder not only of the range of human feeling, but of how that feeling emerges in response to the past as well as the present, and in a universe of others. It promotes an understanding of the fallibility of our assumptions and impositions of self upon the persons of others. It allows us to approach an awareness of the possibilities of others' experience, the myriad means of getting at understanding that, if they do not inspire, will at least bewilder and lead us to marvel at how human beings are able to communicate with each other at all, how it is that they are able to be as certain of love as they are of their misunderstandings and hatreds. If only for this reason, against every accusation of distraction, the diary is worth keeping. ◈

Works Cited

Forster, E. M. *Aspects of the Novel*. San Diego: Harvest—Harcourt Brace Jovanovich, 1985.

Nin, Anaïs. *Incest, From A Journal of Love, The Unexpurgated Diary of Anaïs Nin 1932-1934*. New York: Harcourt Brace Jovanovich, 1992.

----. "The New Woman." *The Mystic of Sex*. Ed. Gunther Stuhlmann. Santa Barbara: Capra Press, 1995. 95-104.

----. *The Novel of the Future*. Athens, OH: Swallow Press-Ohio UP, 1986.

----. and Miller, Henry. *A Literate Passion: Letters of Anaïs Nin and Henry Miller 1932-1953*. Ed. Gunther Stuhlmann. San Diego: Harcourt Brace Jovanovich, Publishers, 1987.

My entire stack of books [diaries], which represents a stack that has been accumulating for years, acts as a strainer. Not the kind of strainer that one uses in the kitchen to strain the soup, but a mental strainer that has a certain charm. All that I say, all that I think, is put slowly through that strainer and spread out on your [diary] pages without any artistic preparation. And there, I study it and I see that by going through the strainer, all of it is improved, purified, filtered. I can remember things that I haven't done so that I wouldn't have the shame of writing them down; but if I did them, I find them written straight out, spread out here with all the love of truth which is not in my character but which you have forced me to cultivate.

So it isn't all egotism, it's also a way of acting as my own teacher (Linotte, 263).

Anaïs Nin

Mirage
From the unpublished diary

June 13, 1940

Desperate at the news. Paris encircled, about to surrender. Ill with pain, sympathy, desire to die with past.

Eduardo [Sanchez, Nin's cousin] is saved. But we only saved our bodies—and the darkness of the world is swallowing us.

Only the human immediate life one still clings to—the last little bits of love and devotion—that is all there is. Everything else is darkness and chaos and horror. Gonzalo upbraids me for not talking like a Marxist—keeping one's vision on the future. The whole world will soon be at war. All of us engulfed—even the innocent ones—so many innocent ones—so many who never caused war. Henry was saying if people [only] behaved all the time with love, generosity, unselfishness—as they do sometimes when death is near.

Gonzalo and I in a little room. In the darkness the dream survives. I tell him I am sad because he wants to be a clochard and I can't be a clocharde. Would you like me to be one? Would you like me to become one? Gonzalo protested vehemently. Said a clochard was alright, but a clocharde was ugly. He liked lovely nails and fine skin and perfumed hair. And I was consoled by this because it seemed to me there was in his vehemence a little condemnation of [his wife] Helba's unkemptness—and I had been thinking how they harmonized—but Gonzalo needs the contrast to himself. I have been feeling the death of our love because of the transformation from passion to love. Gonzalo's bad health made this transition bitter and cruel. I am ten years younger than

---

At the beginning of World War Two, Anaïs Nin and her husband Hugh Guiler were forced to flee France and return to New York City just as she felt herself coming into her own as a writer in Paris. She was soon followed by her lovers, Henry Miller and Gonzalo Moré. Her reunion with them, along with her "exile" in a country with which she had little affinity, left her feeling disillusioned and lost. She subsequently thrust herself into what could be considered an "escapist" love affair with the young artist John Dudley, an affair that not only gave her a temporary reprieve from her sadness, but reawakened her artistic sensibilities.—Ed.

Gonzalo. He is paying for his extravagances, his excesses. He has aged. For three weeks I was tormented by my sensual desires—not satisfied with Henry's possession or Gonzalo's, yearning for violence and fire, dreaming of Negroes, dancing at Harlem to permit this strength to overflow in the drum of the music.

June 16. One night Caresse [Crosby] said: "You *must* meet two young poets who have come all the way from Des Moines to meet you and Miller." I had dinner with Henry first. I thought this would be another bore—young, immature hero-worshipping. I felt lifeless and old. We met first of all [Lafayette] Young, who looked a little like Rank behind his big glasses and who was stuttering with nervousness at meeting us. His worship for John Dudley, his friend, was amazing—complete devotion like a woman's. Then came John, a young man of about thirty looking like a young English aristocrat, tall, blond, beautiful voice. I felt the vitality, the leaping quality, faith, and fervor and craziness, great humility. We looked at his drawings which were interesting. I was not prepared to meet Dudley as an equal—his age separated us at first. I was merely touched by his enthusiasm. Caresse had begged us to be nice to them. I asked them to come see me. I felt his charm. Impulsively I suggested we all go to Harlem because he loves jazz and he is a fine drummer. Instead of dancing we talked, John and I. He was full of vision and penetrations—uncannily so. We sat alone by a window and forgot Harlem. At the end of our talk he said: "I love you" with great warmth and impulsiveness, but it was a love like Durrell's for me. I liked his warmth. The next day he telephoned while we were sitting talking to Eduardo. He was depressed by a day full of failures (he was struggling to get help for a magazine called *Generation*)—could he come? I said come. The four of us went out and sat in a café—came back. By the time he left the force and fire of John moved me. I could only talk to him, dance with him. I was getting a little intoxicated. The next evening when I went to see Henry with Eduardo they were on the watch for me on the stoop (they live next door to Caresse and Henry) and we again spent the evening together, listening to a beautiful talk between Henry and Eduardo which lifted our minds beyond the present—to its cosmic meaning again.

When we returned from the restaurant Henry and Lafayette and Eduardo went to get a beer so John and I had to go up to the room alone—and this I felt like an explosion. I felt his excitement, suspense. I talked to break an unbearable tension. Across the airiness of the conversation, its philosophic rarity, our emotionalism flashed signals at each other. I loved his utter absence of passivity.

The next day Hugh is home. John calls up: "Can I come up and draw your picture?" I say no because we have to go to San Faustino's* housewarming—but would he come with us? He says no. I had said that I might be free to pose and I felt his disappointment. Then Hugh said he was going to play tennis. I could have seen John. I felt that he would call again and come to the San Faustino cocktail with us just to see me. And he did. Then I said, "You can come at five and I can pose for an hour." I knew he was going to come alone. He did. We were tense. He tried to draw. The night before I had noticed he wore a ring too tight for his finger and I said it contracted him, I could not bear it. He took it off and never wore it again—as a symbol of his expansion. We talked but what we really wanted was to kiss. He did not have the courage until we stood by the elevator. We kissed. When we got to San Faustino's house after wandering around dazed—we were absolutely exalted. I forgot about the age. I heard everyone say: we are mourning the past in Paris as the White Russians mourned the old Russia. We are mourning the death of France, of Europe.

John does not feel this death. He is outside of it, as an artist, as a youth. I am sitting and writing a half hour before going to his room. I prayed for a new passion. It comes with the sound of his slender fingers drumming on the table at Harlem, full of sensuality and savagery. He said I was a legend in Des Moines, known for my glamour. He was afraid of me.

Yesterday, after the kiss, I met Gonzalo, who talks only of what he reads in the newspapers, who complains of the heat, of fatigue, of pain, a Gonzalo without fire, dull, heavy, like a sad animal.

June 17. John was looking out for me from his window. He was tense, highly strung, overwhelmed. We talked a little, and then he came over and kissed me. He took all my clothes off. He was amazed by my body. The body of a girl, and yet more than a girl, ageless. I felt him frightened. To tell the truth—I was too, as if this were my first love affair. I was intimidated because I knew what his imagination had made of me—a myth figure. I knew he was overwhelmed and I could not live up to my reputation of the experienced European woman of the world. It was unreal, and I told him so. My own humanness made him at ease, then. I was quiet, timid, passive, feminine. He became impulsive, active, violent. Our caresses were not very good. They were entangled in strangeness.

Kay de San Faustino: Surrealist painter who married Yves Tanguy in August 1940 and painted under the name Kay Sage.—Ed.

69

He was golden, truly Henry's son, a young savage. Same blue eyes, same white skin, laughing face, but a great strength. He is only 26. I pushed aside the literary aura—the past—so that we could breathe. I said this was something happening in space. I wanted life— and there is life in John, [an] abundance of it. At first I feared my age. I am thirty-seven—but when he talked I realized I have no age in his eyes. John said he could tell everybody's age, but not mine. He knew for instance what his wife would look like ten, twenty years from now—but he could not tell about me. He felt I would live forever and that I came out of many lives—far into the past. He said many poetic things—he is full of faith—ardor. Henry and I expanded the world for him. I know this is to be a creation—and I am sad at that—I wanted something else, but I am so grateful for John, for his worship and his youth—and he is a young giant—a force to come. He is full of potentialities. He is explosive, alert, violent, active. He has a strong personality. I enjoy his electric youth. It is better than living in the past and clinging to Gonzalo's heaviness, inertia, to the tragedy of France's death. A few days ago I was dying with France, and with Gonzalo. Today I went again to John's room and forgot all about death. I felt again my own youth. I heard music again. At least my body was not dead. I said to Eduardo I was going to pose for John—and Eduardo said: "It's dangerous. He has his Moon over your Sun."

John says poetic things about my voice. John awake to my hair, my clothes, my skin. There are dangers: John mistaking this for love. He is romantic, idealistic. He knows he carries tomorrow in him. He has no link with Europe or the past. He just has his own new strength. It was his first visit to New York from Des Moines. He called up Caresse one night, drunk, to talk to her about the magazine. She said: "Come and see me." Caresse is living with Canada Lee, and has promised to take me to Harlem. Is the current of life set in motion again, by John? He cannot sleep with the excitement. He is tender, worshipful.

June 23. I went to him every afternoon this week. At first it was like a game, an electric game. We passed the phase of unreality. The second time I responded sensually. He delighted me, with his fervor, his new found strength. I felt his awakening, his gratitude, his chivalry, his romanticism, his excitement. It was contagious. I came always dancing with a beating heart. I left after a bath of love. The second afternoon, when I left him, I felt my own gayety stronger than death. The dawns in his eyes, the wonder.

I met Gonzalo. And then of course, when I was sad to be liberated of the obsession with Gonzalo, it happened, that he was amorous again because I was turning away. Gonzalo began to pursue me again.

Gonzalo was desirous and asking for a whole night with me—because I broke away after suffering torture at his lack of passion. One afternoon after being with John, I went to Henry. We went out together for dinner. I had said many things to John about living on the peaks, how he needed only intensity, that his going away would not matter, that this was a violent dream in space. Then as I was having dinner with Henry in the Chinese restaurant, they came in, the boys. I felt a pang of pleasure and then a pang of pain at the thought of losing him. They have no money, no one has sponsored his magazine. They have to go home to Des Moines. And I cannot help them. Someone gave them a little money. They stayed a few more days, until Monday now.

Strange boy. He is a descendent of the Earl of Dudley, the favorite of Queen Elizabeth, of Thomas Dudley, Duke of Yorkshire. His family owned Kenilworth, of Walter Scott's novels, which once enchanted me. And that is how he looks, like a darling of women, a fighter, a tyrant, reckless, courageous, romantic, a figure out of a novel. Fine, tall, white body, hair around his head like a faun's, curled and golden. Half artist. He is a good artist. Marvelous drawings, with character. Aware, awake, alert, luminous. Near him, after I tell myself I do not love him, I feel a sensual warmth. He asks me to say I love him: I have not said it. I act as if I did. I came to him in the middle of a violent storm once. I came to him on Sunday when I am usually a prisoner. He says wonderful things. He is extraordinarily aware. He sees me. His drawings of me are accurate, interesting. He has impulses of protection. Asks if I have been hurt living with Henry. Asks what he can do for me. I said: "You rescued me from death. One rescue in a week, is it not enough?" When he feels unequal to me I say: "Can you say you are less than me only because I was in China and you were not?" He says: "You accept me. You challenge my strength and make me whole. I feel stronger with you. At the same time I feel weaker than before other women. I was an egoist. I did not consider woman...not as an equal." He has a small, childish, dreamy wife, married only for a year. She is even sexually too small for him. Too small. No giant. He will be someone. He will be loved by women, by everybody. He is already. People listen to him. A miracle may happen. He is a conqueror, in a way. He is determined. His hesitancies are only youthful. He has strong hatreds and strong loves, vitality. I see him as light and joy. His worship revives me, so that I returned to Gonzalo full of charm, fancies, without this tightness and bitterness of absolute dependence, the poisonous acrid fears. I returned nonchalant, imaginative, and he fell in love with me all over again, and took my clothes off and made love to me all over the body as I like it. I'm like a drunkard, drunk on loves, spending most of my life in bed, an orgy of caresses. Mad, absolutely mad. Lying with all of them, and creating, laughing, inventing, writing. Liberated, liberated of the fears which made me clutch at Gonzalo. What pain these last months. Watching the passion die, and then replenishing at the source of love itself, a tender, young, passionate love—and drinking there—and feeling John gaining strength, sexually, spiritually, emotionally, in one week. The miracle. And everything around it is nourished by the miracle, life transfusion of love given to all. I asked John: "Have you the courage to live something inhuman, the poem?" But as I leave him I see pain in his face and I yield to a human impulse and say: "You know, there is no more passion between Henry and me."

Henry took us all last night to 662 Briggs Avenue in Brooklyn where he lived nine years of his childhood. We walked through it all, he recollecting. John at my side, silent. Jealous? The night was beautiful. The past so rich and bursting full, and the present John, walking together.

What John and I tied together were two quick pulsing rhythms, quickening blood, adventure.

I have infinite patience with his stuttering, his youthful errors. I say to him when he retracts or apologizes: "Never retract with me." When he stumbles, hesitates: "Go on." He asks: "Is that clear? Do you understand?" I said: "Don't write. You are a painter." He only wearies me when he has to make it a great love—instead of hunger, electricity sparkles, all but love. When he tries to carry me to see if he can CARRY ME AWAY FROM ALL THE OTHERS.

He has no past, but I had no future, so we exchanged. And I feel light and strange. I listen to my own young faith speaking words of generosity. I thought I could never be free for one moment of Gonzalo's hair around me. As I had to get free of Henry, a necessary separateness. Eduardo had been saying: "You have no center of gravity. You live outside of yourself, in your relationships. You are really mad, in a way. Hugh is your only basis. But that may be wonderful—for poetry. You seek only the peaks."

So grateful I am to John—that I can feel, laugh, vibrate again. He said to me: "Henry has something of death in him—Hugh too. But you are of a different color altogether. I see a greyness in them, but you are barbaric red." As an artist he sees me beautiful. I see the translucence of his skin, shadowless. I like creating him sensually. I unleash. I feel his body as if I were making it with my own hands touching off new cells of responses, new sparks, inflaming, opening. He leaps in my hands. The flames again.

He is full of delicacies. I spoil others so, my love is so active, I have not known this being served and adored like a Princess. He says when I go down the street he wants to push everyone away so I can walk down alone, guarded by him alone. When he says romantic things (almost like the ones I said to Henry) I laugh gently, mockingly, a soft laughter. He said after our first afternoon: "This room is now immortalized." Sensually he is learning; he was fumbling at first. But he is gifted for nuances, he is gifted for love-making. Can I bear his going away? Will I miss his caresses, his exaltation. He does not sleep. He spends his nights making drawings of me. I did betray Gonzalo— oh, not by sleeping with John, I do not consider these acts betrayals— betrayal is when I brought John a piece of Japanese wood Gonzalo stole for me once, to light and produce the most unique incense perfume. Which Gonzalo and I only burned for ourselves, to make strange hotel rooms smell like us. That is betrayal. Stealing what belongs to the other, to the very soul of the relationship, and desecrating it. My sensual gift is only a great expansion of the self drawing on new words, new sense, for a new experience, another self totally unrelated to Gonzalo. I dedicated *House of Incest* to both John and his wife, of which I am not at all jealous, which touched him. He places her under my protection. When I was sixteen, I used to read Kenilworth with passion. It had a magic meaning. I shall call John "Kenilworth." "John" I do not like because of the other John,* because it is too simple.

I often can cut through the manifestations of anger and recognize the suffering behind it. Many people react to suffering with anger.

For death and disintegration you require a passivity like Henry's and Gonzalo's—which I do not have. Even in small things. Gonzalo does not know when he is hot or cold. He goes out for a week in the same costume. If it is light and the weather changes he gets a grippe. He suffers the grippe. Waits. He suffers Hugh's presence—my removals or withdrawals, equally. He waits. Does not rebel. One day I say: "Gonzalo you're so hot in that suit. You're suffering. I saw fine looking slacks there with light shirts." We go and look at them. I urge him to get them. It is I who had to help them both to find an apartment. I urge them into more expensive places because I do not want to thrust them into a drab past again, into dark rooms. And neither one can bear the places which remind them of past hungers and pains they underwent, due to their passivity.

July 4. Orienta Apartments. Mamaroneck. Once I said to John: "The Hindus marry and then they wait ten days during which they court

---

John Erskine, with whom Nin had a failed love affair. A complete account can be found in Early Diary 4.*—Ed.*

their wives." We were talking about John's begging for time. He didn't want to go until he had really possessed me. And strangely enough, it took ten days, and the tenth day he was gone.

A strange, terrifying thing has happened to me twice now. As soon as I feel the downward curve of love I throw myself into a new one. This time I threw myself into desire for John, a meeting of two fires. After our fourth afternoon together he asked me: "You have never said you loved me." We were separated for two days. During those two days he was like a wild horse suddenly corralled. He rebelled against my power over him. No woman had ever touched off such deep responses, sensually, imaginatively. Until now he had been the loved one. And here I took hold of his body and soul without even saying: "I love you!" On one of those nights of rebellion, he saw the film "La Femme du Boulanger." He saw the handsome shepherd whom the woman eats like a beautiful fruit. John asked himself if that was all he was to me. Those two days I was away with Hugh, and John was to wait until Monday to see me again before leaving. In his rebellion against my power he decided not to wait. He cried out: "It hurts, it hurts." It was a storm of revolt against the wounding pain of passion. He would leave before I returned, but he had to wait. It was Monday morning. He was talking with Henry. Henry said: "Anaïs is coming later." My name struck John like a bombshell. He had to wait. Then I came. He told me all he had suffered. Still I did not say I loved him. We plunged into caresses. His were violent, hungry. I liked the fire in him. I bathed in it.

All the time I knew it was not love. But I caught fire to his own fire, and once I did say the word he was begging for, and I was even deceived by my desire. Came the last day, when we possessed each other like savages. The last evening when we all went out together to Chinatown, Hugh, Eduardo, Lafayette, John and I. As we walked the streets I was drunk with desire. He was exalted. We wanted desperately to touch each other again. It was a torture. I could not let him go away. I felt on the point of doing something mad. The fire was too strong. We were intoxicated. I promised to see him again. I persuaded Hugh not to leave. I saw John. And suddenly, it was all unreal, the exaltation died down. I did not feel his departure. I felt nothing. Detached. The drunkenness left me. I fell into an abyss. Back to the familiar loves, to human life, grey days, sickness, bad moods, fatigue, to aging and dying, to sorrowing over a lost world. John left me nothing of his goldenness, not a tremor of desire. All a mirage.

I do not want to see him again.

I cannot remember his words. Nothing he said left an echo. No caress left its imprint on the blood. A mirage.

Hugh and I came to this place for him, so that he can enjoy his boating and fishing. I hate it. I shall have to run away from it.

I felt much more the separation from Gonzalo for four days of Hugh's holidays than I did parting from John.

Tonight lying in bed hating my bourgeois life, feeling desperate and destructive while Americans celebrate the Fourth of July throwing whistling bombs which remind me of those which terrorized us in Europe.

Impasse. I should accept twilight, deserts, impasses. I am only liberated of my obsessional love but not of the love.

July 13. After four days in Mamaroneck with Hugh I spent a night with Gonzalo and took the plane to Richmond, Virginia for Bowling Green saying to Gonzalo I was meeting Hugh in Washington. Gonzalo came to see me off after a close and emotional night.

At Richmond Henry was expecting me, with John Payne, Caresse's young lover. We got to Hampton Manor, the enchanted House of the Grand Meaulne, the enchanted house of Louveciennes, with its white columns, its deep frame of old trees, its large harmonious rooms, its extraordinary stillness, to the tune of whip o'wills, enchanted sleep.

Caresse, whose portrait by Max Ernst was a curled frilled flower heart which might have been a starched undulating ruffled petticoat, a ballet skirt molded into stiff seashell waves by a desirous thumb. A starched open flower heart petticoat—a ballet. Such is Caresse's interior. A ballet. Though she stutters because she is made to speak with caresses only, I knew she loved and loved everything and it is only men she embraces passionately. Her ballet draws everybody around her. Her life at the Mill* was spangled with all the personalities of her time (that was the place where I pretended to be going when I stayed all night away from Hugh). With Henry and I at Hampton Manor this life, she felt, might repeat itself. When she saw us there, writing, talking, she felt she had already lived this. Or perhaps it was the Mill again, with Harry Crosby like a meteor, with Breton, Eluoard, Frank Crane, Ernst, the painters, the aristocrats, the wealthy, the capricious. So many currents in Caresse's receptive being that she becomes the central link, and everywhere she brings forth friendships, other links, currents are started by her life force. And she sits stuttering, rubbing her eyes, rubbing smooth the wrinkles on her face, flicking her tongue, her small sensual pink tongue. We slept through long hot afternoons. Henry

---

Le Moulin du Soleil, an estate near Ermenonville, outside of Paris.—Ed.

wrote in the morning, adding many pages to the second volume of *Capricorn.*[*]

We had received telegrams from the Earl of Dudley that he might arrive Thursday or Friday with his wife. I was not stirred. Yet when Thursday evening came and Caresse took us off to the movies I did say: "Dudley will arrive tonight."

Henry said: "No, at three A.M." Caresse said: "Tomorrow."

So we went to the movies. But I knew. As we were driving back to the house in the darkness I said: "They are there. I know it." They were.

As soon as I heard John's voice the sensual turmoil reawakened. His wife is small, dead, insignificant, lifeless. John stole a kiss in the dark stairway. And then we all went to bed. Henry and I in one room, John and his wife, Caresse alone because Payne is now in the army. I lay awake desiring John whom I do not love, wishing he had the audacity to rise in the middle of the night, imagining how it would feel to meet in the dark, secretly, feeling each other's bodies, as I read long ago in a novel which stirred me erotically at the age of nine. Darkness and nakedness. In the morning the current of desire between us was so strong that is was unendurable. And I was leaving in the afternoon for ten days. And John's wife followed him every minute with a fear of me. But Caresse took destiny in her own hands. She took John's wife in her car to shop one hour away. Henry was trying to get in touch with his friend Emil at Fredericksburg. I suggested lightly that he too go to town and telephone as I wanted to see Emil (not true). Henry did it. John had just finished taking a shower. The tension was so acute that as I entered his room and he began to kiss me hungrily in front of the window while we watched them driving away, a storm broke for the second time during our caresses, a violent electric storm. I stood by the window. John behind me. I pressed against him and felt his desire so hard and strong, while he opened my blouse, took my breasts in his two hands and pushed them upward as if to drink from them. Storm over our head, all the peace gone, fire and lightning bolts through the body. We threw ourselves on the bed and he took me with violence.

How grateful I was to Caresse for this moment, Caresse with her knowledge of passion. How joyous I was to have discovered this joy divorced from the pangs of love, this purely sensual vibration which altered in no way my deep love for Gonzalo. A vibration which takes place when John is there, a drunkenness which lasts only while he is there, and of which I am free as soon as I leave him, free of love. Yes, he is the shepherd and all I want is to bite into him when he is there,

---

[*]*This book evolved into* Sexus.*—Ed.*

flesh so alive, the summer perspiration fresh as dew—the sensual underlip. He is alive. Electric joys.

Nothing else about him interests me. Atmosphere of Middle West America homeliness. The cult of the ugly. The drinking. His dream and talk. I cannot even remember them. Absolutely ordinary, youthful. Too simple. He is imitating Henry. So when I leave him, the spell is broken. I am free.

Caresse and I in the airplane, talking, confiding. Caresse thought Hugh was going to meet me, but I told her Hugh did not know I was arriving. Gonzalo was going to meet me. Poor Gonzalo was desperately anxious—we were an hour late due to the fog. He was waiting for me on the curb, anxiously staring at all the taxis. We spent the night in our little room. The next day we came together to Mamaroneck, to look for a place for him and Helba, near us. But they are so slow they will move in by the time I am ready to leave. Here I have no excitement or fever. So I fall into an abysm. The smallest frustration makes me despondent. If I am thwarted I can easily think of suicide. It seems to me that all I want now is adventure, adventure, adventure. And I have not the strength for it. After the ten days of orgies with John and the tension, I broke down. I was glad when he left. Each time I have to withdraw—broken. And yet I am full of desire, restlessness, fever, hunger.

This place: a bourgeois apartment house near the Bay. Everything genteel and well regulated. The husbands all go to the city in the morning. The beaches are dull. The people stodgy and uninterested in each other. It is all plain and homely and tidy and colorless.

Now I think coldly like a demon: John will help me get through the summer. I will get strong. And in the fall I will throw myself into the fullest, most hectic life possible. I must find another love. I must get free of Gonzalo. It is all painful and negative now. He weighs on me heavily now. I am only made for passion. The temperature of love I cannot endure. I am afraid. I think it is death. Everything but passion seems [like] death to me. Only in fever do I feel life.

One word from Gonzalo, one careless word, can darken my whole day. His bad health, his laziness, his self-mutilations, negativism. When we were looking for a place, before we enter, he says: "There is nothing here." I say: "How do you know?" I enter. I ask. There is something. Then he will postpone his answer, and lose it.

July 28. On the train from Fredericksburg to New York. In Hampton Manor again, but Flo follows John like a shadow every minute. We cannot even talk to each other alone. We cannot touch each other. Tuesday, Wednesday. He does not know ruse yet. At night when we walk—we sway in the dark to touch each other's hands. Powerful currents traverse us. At any moment we could make a wild gesture. The excitement mounts and becomes a pain. The body aches with desire. John feels it. One afternoon we went to the Potomac River to swim. When I walked towards John in my bathing suit I saw the desire on his face. We have to act. Only Thursday morning Flo was not well and she let John drive the poor Negro with a tumor on his finger, to take him to the doctor. We sat in a café and stole kisses. The tension grew so keen that I wanted to scream. This morning the great heat discouraged Henry from coming with us to the Village and Flo did not come. We took the Negro to the doctor, and then we drove to a pine forest I had observed on the way. We entered into the heart of it, walking on pine needles. Then we kissed voraciously. What strength in John's hands, what firmness. He slipped his hands into my shirt. I felt his desire hard. We lay on the pine needles. We almost shouted with the wildness of it, the ecstasy. Then we returned to the house, gentle and appeased. When Henry and Flo took a siesta, John and I went down to the cellar, to the Mexican room, where he wanted me to see his drawings. But we could not talk very long. I was naked under my cotton dress. He bit my thighs. Again delirium. The last day—only one hour together. Unable to unleash our desire for each other, I was forced to notice John's character, and I saw the points at which we touch, sensuality, electric tensions, positive unrushing natures, a likeness of temperament, swift, proud, domineering, active. Capacity to burn. Now he has a timid, plaintive, shrunken wife who wants him small, who is afraid of the violence in him, and a mistress who gives him a tremendous sense of expansion, sets him on fire, challenges all his forces. The first time John and I returned from the ride in the village, she was weeping—and she said, without knowing anything, but out of pure intuition: "I was thinking how it would be if someday you loved somebody else." The day of their marriage she had already lost him. John was already beyond his marriage. He calls her the waif.

Strange thing. Wanting to reassure Henry I took a siesta with him knowing he would take me and I responded fully.

And it was after this I went down to the Mexican room and could still vibrate under John's earthy caresses.

Mars of the earth again.

John can do something none of my other loves could do—he can make me feel free of pain, joyous, sensual.

I enjoy my power.

I can say his name in such a way that he says it is like a knife. I can make him tremble with desire, shake with it, keep him awake, tortured. He has given what woman should value highly—a young man's first passion, so total, so romantic and fervent. I feel beautiful, desirable, potent in his hands. The light in his face at times is dazzling. After the walk in the dark when merely brushing each other we could create ecstasy, even, in the dark his face was resplendent.

John, it is marvelous to arouse desire. Do not be too hurt. So much in the world we should caress and love only with the blood and the flesh because it is beautiful, brilliant, alive—as we love fire. No small role—giving me pure joy—life in the body, this miraculous current without pain. For the first time the Sun. I was never given the sun.

Poor little Flo—she taps his knee lightly—with a small, helpless hand. I dig my nails into them and John trembles like a racehorse.

Aug. 12. Mamaroneck. I believe I have defended myself against loving John, and *suffering*. I believe that just as [in] the beginning [when] I still loved Henry and couldn't yield to Gonzalo absolutely, so have I defended myself against feeling John. Whenever I arrive at Hampton Manor I am prepared not to feel. And so the last time. Because there was Flo, there were obstacles, because John is poor and not free, because of his youth… Anyway, I arrived cold. And for a few hours all is well. But soon the warmth comes. John may be talking. I see his eyes on me. I look at his mouth. Near his temples the blond hair curls like a child's.

The next day the torments begin. I found him depressed. Flo attacked him each time they got into their room. Her instinct is not blind. She tells him: "I am not the woman for you. Anaïs is the woman for you." And then, more obscurely, she fights to diminish him, crush him. She tells him he must not be crude (when he is merely impulsive), that he talks too much. Or she attacks his work. Poor John.

All the time we are watching for a moment together. All through the first day it was impossible. The next day Caresse arrived early in the morning. She sent us on errands which included two huge valises so no one else could get into the car. John and I went—and we went to the woods. The moment was so short, that I could not respond fully in spite of my excitement, but I remember the starved kisses, the violence. That evening walk in the dark and sparks burning through us.

That was a great day. Caresse announced her partner publisher was failing her. Somehow or other we all simultaneously began to talk about doing it all ourselves. Caresse was very concrete and determined. We sat at lunch planning to run a press in Hampton Manor to publish the books she had intended to do: *Nadja* [by] Breton translated by Jolas, a novel of Kay Boyle's, Memoirs of Marianne Gold, Cendrars, Radiquet, etc.

We walked over to the barn, but found it was too open for the press. We could not get it heated later. Then we walked to the house built for the servants, a lovely little white house all of natural wood inside, with many rooms. We decided to install the press there. As this was shaping into a solution of John's life (penniless—nowhere to go— a good craftsman—he could live on running the press), it became all intermingled with our love. John saw it as *our* work, I saw him working incited by his love—and the excitement took the form of an intense personal joy which we wanted desperately to share together, to share together like a bottle of wine. While everybody was looking through the rooms, talking, I caught John alone walking behind me. I turned fully on him and whispered: "I love you!" which completely set him on fire.

That evening we could not talk, we were so full of emotions. John is so different from Gonzalo—so creative and not twisted. Things take form in his hands. He loves to build. He loves to work, invent, discover. The night before we had talked about—Henry arguing against us—the necessity of recreating the universe from the beginning with our own hands. John has that. He likes to dominate matter. This likeness in us attracts us—this capability. That night the accord between our temperament was so visible that Flo left the table and went to her room.

Next morning. It is the day of my departure. We find ourselves alone in the library sitting far away from each other because we are in a turmoil and John says he wants to pounce on me. Every time we look at each other we feel we are reeling. The world is reeling around us. It is unbearable. John comes over to me, takes my face in both his hands and quickly covers it with kisses.

He is despondent. He feels defeated, imprisoned by Flo, frustrated. I am depressed too, from so much control and repression.

A little later when I am all packed I find Henry has fallen asleep. I leave the room. I go to Caresse and ask her if she will call John for me (Flo is ill in bed) so that I may see him a little while. She suggests I go to the pavilion and wait there. She'll come with John later. And this she does so deftly Flo thinks John has been called to help Caresse carry things to the pavilion where the press is to be.

She leaves us there. My heart is beating. We kiss. John is ecstatic. "Everything you do I love, everything. You are perfect, marvelous! I like your audacity. I like all your impulses. Now I am happy."

In the train I travel with Henry who has to go to N.Y. I don't know if it is Henry who has changed or my image of him, but he seems faded, grey somehow. In the train I am anxious because I have felt John more than other times and I am going to fall in love with him. There are reserves in my desire for John which did not exist in my other loves. Even now, the night before I left for Virginia—lying with Gonzalo— after his possession of me—he moved his head in such a way that his long black hair brushed my breasts, and this brushing of Gonzalo's hair over my breast I felt so deeply, as if every strand of hair were tangled with a strand of my own hair, and tied around a cell of my blood.

John's gestures do not have this vibration on me. The intoxication is there each time, the need to embrace, kiss, lie with him—but only while he is there and it does not grow roots into my being. Even this time, though I remember the intoxication, I do not feel those blood roots stirring in me which makes a woman know the man is inside her womb as a child would be, stirring at the center of her being.

Aug. 22. Saturday I discovered I was pregnant—three months! Days of anguish over the money and the complications I feared. [Dr.] Jacobson put me in the hands of a good German Jew who works for rich women. He said it would have to be done in two operations, one to insert the bag which dilates the womb (this is done without ether) and then the final one done with ether. I set the date for the 21st, Wednesday. Arrived at 9:30. Was strapped like an insane person, even wrists tied, arms, waist, legs. A strange sensation of utter helplessness. Then the doctor came in. As he began to work he found the womb dilating so easily that he continued the operation, in spite of the terrific pain. And so in six minutes of torture I had done what is usually done with ether! But it was over. I couldn't believe it. Hugh so full of anguish, and Gonzalo. And today I am home, lying down most of the time.

Gonzalo came to make lunch.

I missed my trip to Virginia. But I didn't suffer from that. The only wonderful moment in all this was when I was lying on a little cot in the doctor's office, and another woman came. The nurse pulled the curtain so that I could not see her. She was made to undress and lie down— relax. The nurse left us. Soon I heard a whisper to me: "How was it?" I reassured her—told her how I had been able to bear it without ether, so it would be nothing with ether.

She said: "How long were you pregnant?"

"Three months."

"I only two—but I'm scared. My husband is away. He doesn't know. He must never know."

I couldn't explain to her that my husband knew, but that my lover had to be deceived and made to believe I had no relations with Hugh. Lying there whispering about the pain—I never felt such a strong kinship with woman—woman—this one I could not see, or identify, the one who was also lying in a cot filled with primitive fear and an obscure sense of murder, or guilt, and of an unfair struggle against nature—an unequal struggle with all the man-made laws against us, endangering our lives, exposing us to inexperienced maneuvers, to being economically cheated and morally condemned—woman truly the victim now, beyond the help of her courage and aliveness. How much is to be said against the ban on abortion. What a tragedy this incident becomes for the woman. At this moment she is hunted down, really. The doctor is ashamed, deep down, falsely so. Society condemns him. Everything goes on in an atmosphere of crime and trickery. And the poor woman who was whispering to me, afterwards, I heard her say to the doctor: "Oh, doctor, I'm so grateful to you, so grateful!" That woman moved me so much. I wanted to know her. I wanted to pull the curtain and see her. But I realized she was all women—the humility, the thoughtfulness, the fear and the childlike moment of utter defenselessness. A pregnant woman is already a being in anguish. Obscurely each pregnancy is a conflict. The break is not simple. You are tearing off a fragment of flesh and blood. Added to this deeper conflict is the anguish, the quest for the doctor, the fight against exploitation, the atmosphere of underworld bootlegging, a racket. The abortion is made a humiliation and a crime. Why should it be? Motherhood is a vocation like any other. It should be freely chosen, not imposed upon woman.

Aug. 26. Days of convalescence. Gonzalo's behavior restored my faith and calmed my doubts. Finally today as we were resting side by side I felt his desire stirring and he placed my hand over it and let me caress him until he came in my hand. And I was all warmed by his desire. I am in love with Gonzalo still. I know it now.

Since I have returned from Virginia we have been close again. In utter despair at American surroundings, the emptiness, the homeliness, we began to dream Paris all over again. He told me one story after another... I urged him to write them. He recreated the atmosphere for me. The little I had seen myself ([Hans] Reichel, Artaud) began to expand in my own imagination. Listening to Gonzalo and remembering I began to write, started with the pages on the rue Dolent,* a fantastic story about Reichel. With Gonzalo I abstracted myself from the American scene. It was a collaboration. After working I often telephone him and tell him: "Look what you have done! It is your book." His stories are terrifying. I live in the nightmare, now, started to write

---

*A short story Nin began in Paris and continued in New York. See The Diary of Anaïs Nin, Vol. 2, pp. 229-230, and Vol. 3, pg. 46.—Ed.

flowingly last week, two days after the abortion. I was working again. Yesterday I wrote the pages on the café. I am working welding it all, the barge story, the rag pickers.

A corrupt man is like a woman. Corruption is a kind of passivity, a pregnable, open, yielding element which attracts one. One feels like raping, mastering, plunging into it, into this corrupt, lax, open being through which all currents flow. Corruption is an opening, an openness. During Gonzalo's telling of stories I suffer sometimes to see the expression of yieldingness, of abandon, which took him everywhere... the abandon... That must be the way a man feels about woman, the desire to insert into this soft, open flesh, the hard erect knife of his will and desire.

Poor John. I think of him now as the brightest son I ever had but I love the dark one best of all, the one who has shown ugliness, envy, fear, weakness, criminal negligence, corruption. Corruption is shown by the choice of ambiance, and Gonzalo's choice was of the darkest, most diseased and corrupt of all, the monsters.

Aug. 27. Strange days—of loneliness, barrenness and inner burning. I live absolutely in the past and partly in Gonzalo's past. We meet like conspirators, while Hugh is fishing, and we talk, talk, talk. Then I work. Physically I am at a very low ebb, weak. But spiritually I carry a demon of restlessness, hunger, imaginings. I want a rich, multiple, dazzling life. I want abundance, recklessness, sumptuousity and the heights of passion, up to the stake. I want to be burned, to be burned. And now I want to live out everything within the very layers at which I am creating. I have set the climate and I must find it. Where?

Sept. 1. I must beware of my imagination. At the moment when the love becomes neutral, I begin to suffer from doubts. Gonzalo, on the contrary, has nestled in this love and is full of trustingness. Gonzalo does not expect catastrophe now. He expected it during the passion. I expect it now. Doubt has grown in me, and has made me suffer all this year. Last night I told Hugh I was leaving for Virginia at midnight and I arranged to have dinner with Gonzalo in New York. I told him I could leave or not leave, as he wanted. He didn't say anything, so I finally began to talk to him telling him how because of his passivity I had suffered and that I was detaching myself from him. He was immensely surprised and he laughed good naturedly, absolutely innocently. He said all I seemed to be missing was his tyranny, and that he had changed deeply and felt more balanced, less crazy than before, that he believed in me now. I said I loved our rhythm before when he took the active role, that now I was lost. Gonzalo explained that all men were stupid when it was a question of ruse, and that he had grown to depend on my ruses for our meetings. He showed great tenderness but I did realize the change, and I feel that this Gonzalo I don't like, that I preferred the crazy one who made scenes. This Gonzalo is old, fat, peaceful. But I have become aware of the demon in me who is the cause of my suffering, the demon of doubt. This doubt may cause me to destroy the very love I want, as I destroyed my life with Henry because of it, because fundamentally, Henry having made his love of June the theme of his work, I never really believed in his love. And Gonzalo being enslaved by Helba's helplessness, her deafness, I feel equally that in the end when the passion is over I may lose him. I have a feeling I should make Gonzalo jealous as I made Henry jealous, by running away to New York. But that only reassures me for a little while and then Henry's egotism destroyed my faith again. They clutch and cling and howl when I leave them but how badly they love.

It is all my fault. I love with so much devotion that I make everybody selfish... I know there is something very wrong with me. I need proof of love constantly and that is wrong and cruel for others.

Sunday all day I tortured myself, needlessly, with doubts. Monday morning I didn't telephone Gonzalo. Then he telephoned me to say that because of the hurricane he thought I should not leave for Virginia. He was afraid for me. Such a small thing can make me happy for a day and then an equally small act of thoughtlessness can plunge me into despair.

To rise beyond the emotional weakness, I worked well last week. Then Henry came and read what I had done and his criticism was negative. He had nothing to say about the fragments themselves, and all he could see was that they were not woven together. He said it was bad, monotonous and static. This stopped my writing completely. I showed it to Gonzalo then. He responded. But why should I depend on such responses? Why must I depend on others for everything, never on myself? I am back to where I was years ago, before analysis, to a devouring and doubting, continuous hyper-sensitivity and fears. What can I do now? Before I was helped by Allendy and then by Rank. Now I have to heal myself alone. At least I realize it is all in my imagination. But the suffering is there, continuous, haunting, like an infection. No relief. A few hours of peace, and then the gnawing begins again.

Anaïs, stop devouring and fearing. You are a tortured being—all your life. Come out of this darkness and live passionately again, forgetting yourself. Create. You isolate yourself with your love and you watch every nuance and every word and every gesture. It is bad. You must be courageous and ruthless and reckless. If you need always a new love because you only believe in the new, you will lose Gonzalo whom you still love. Gonzalo.

Sept. 5. Hampton Manor all changed by the petty antagonisms grown between Mrs. Salvador Dalí and Henry and John. She is grasping, used them (she doesn't know English), appropriated the library where we used to talk, the salon where Dalí works. Meals were full of hostility and mockery. The house is run for Dalí and the wife wants it run like Dalí's kingdom, and we his subjects. John and Flo feel humiliated by the conversations in French, John critical of Dalí's persistent work and gayety (he whistles and sings all day). I would not have felt all this. I am less rebellious at helping, or being used. John hates to serve. Henry hated Mrs. Dalí's cuddling of Dalí. They hated everything and made crazy statements like: Dalí only eats lamb, as if this were in itself a crime. Henry resorted to his maniacal contradictions. I liked to hear Dalí talk but it was impossible. John was jealous when I talked Spanish. Mrs. Dalí was on guard against me. Dalí liked me and lost his shyness and retiringness when I came. He showed me his work.

But Hampton Manor the enchanted had vanished. John had suffered so much from my absence and the fear that I should die that he was growling at everything. His money was finished. He had to go home. The press plan was abandoned because Caresse did not have the money for it. John would have to do all the work, and I didn't want it because I don't want to leave Gonzalo and in Hampton Manor I could not be with John.

But again John and I sat in the same room, garden or road, felt each other's presence like wild magnets, and the intoxication began anew. We only had one walk together, the last day, John telling me how he suffered when I was away, how he came to life when I arrived, how he wanted me. What power throws us together, makes me forget Gonzalo. Desire. Desire. Again our eyes fixed on each other each time Henry and Flo are not looking, and we hypnotize each other completely and fall into the well of the other's being, compelled, blind, drunk. His blue eyes are firm, fixed like a virile possession. He takes me. At other times he is dissolved with desire, his voice grows huskier and warm and I feel bathed in warmth and passion.

We planned to meet in N.Y.—to spend nights together.

In the evening when we parted at midnight Flo was in her room, Henry in the bathroom, I ran downstairs lightly because I heard John locking the doors. He heard me coming. We stood for an instant in the darkness of the porch, crackling and burning like wild torches, he all gold and blue, I all in red and black—hearts snapping with the tension, whispering love words. Lover. He the lover—feverish with desire, the voice and laughter of the lover, the man one wants to be locked in a room with.

I am grateful to have a lover I want to be locked with in a room—a lover on fire.

I sit in the train and I still feel him, where one should feel a lover. He says I am his only joy. I say he is my only joy. He says I am the only one who has his rhythm. I say you have mine.

The day of his birthday we found a pack of cards fallen around the car. I picked up the ones with their faces turned upward. I do not know their meaning. The Negress said it was all lucky.

Sad days, the last of Hampton Manor. We see the long, long roads before us. From afar they look wet. From near they are absolutely dry. Mirage. Many branches of the trees lie wrapped in cocoons of spider webs, dead leaves and dead insects lying tangled in the gown of white fog ribbons, the maternal fluid weaving its cocoon pockets in the forest, silvery envelopes, snowy white wigs of crystallized saliva. The earth is sienna colored. The Negro is singing on his horse. There is a pool crowded with headless trees. Dalí is painting a guitar that is loose and slack like a body without nerves and a woman's body taut like a guitar while the hand plays on her sex. Dalí is painting a horse whose insides contain a woman whose child is kissing his horse teeth while the child's enormous horse-like sex hangs limp. Henry is writing about Greece. John is writing about corruption and rebelling: "Why do we take up your death theme? We haven't died." Why indeed, the gold sun youth of America wallowing in our European death chant.

"Well can you visualize tomorrow?" I asked. "You are tomorrow."

"I can't—it's true."

So they chant death with us.

Sept. 7. I am afraid to ask myself what John will be for me—he will be my joy for how long? John—absolutely poor—and unwilling to submit to the discipline of a job—because he wants the life of the artist. John imprisoned by his wife's complete dependence and clutching love like Helba's for Gonzalo—helplessness, weakness, dependence. She has no life of her own—no creation, no activity. She lives vicariously through him—a shadow—his shadow—his echo.

I am cornered. John is not the man. When will *he* come? Will he have the savour of Gonzalo, with strength? Will I have to give all the strength again? Until I die? I await him. In this mood exactly I awaited Gonzalo a few months before he came. I knew then he would be big, and not from France—I almost felt him. I saw his eyes in Fez. Now— Jean de la Lune had said watch out for 1940. It cannot be John.

I think I am a little mad, with feeling, with awareness, with obstacles. Create, Anaïs. Every word you wrote was always the gold key which opened the doors of your prison. The Lawrence book brought you Henry. The *House of Incest* Gonzalo. The *Winter of Artifice* John. It is your female chant for man, for the lover. Write. It is your ornament, your grace, your seduction, your chant for courting. Create, Anaïs. He will come. ◈

John Dudley at Hampton Manor
Photo © Anaïs Nin Trust

Toyoko Yamamoto

Examining *Anaïs Nin no Shôjo Jidai*
Sumiko Yagawa's Anaïs Nin as a Young Girl

For those familiar with Anaïs Nin's writings, it is not difficult to picture her as a *japonisante*. Nin often mentions her rereading Lady Murasaki's work as much she does that of Proust. Nin writes in her *Diary of Anaïs Nin, Vol. 7*: "...one of my most important childhood readings was a volume on Japan from a collection, *Voyage Autour du Monde*" (5). The publication of the Japanese version of *A Spy in the House of Love* translated by Koji Nakata gave Nin an opportunity to visit Japan in 1966 and her essay entitled "Women and Children of Japan" from *In Favor of the Sensitive Man*—excerpted from *Diary 7*—reflects Nin's respect for Japanese sensitivity and aesthetics. Despite her appreciation for Japanese values, she was not satisfied with the limited number of books written by Japanese women that had been translated into English by the 1960s and the early 1970s.

In *Collages*, Nin uses the traditional Japanese kimono as a metaphor to represent the people's isolation from liberation: "Nobuko was bound in her enveloping kimono, the wide sleeves like closed wings against her body, the feet in white cotton and sandals, seeking to shake off the ritualistic past, the thoughtful meditative forms, the contained stylizations, and she wondered whether she could emerge from centuries of confinement" (82). This also reminds me of the Japanese doll on the fireplace mantel in Nin's Los Angeles house that I saw when I visited Rupert Pole there in the early spring of 1983. The glass case that had previously surrounded the doll in real kimono fabric had been removed to save the doll from suffocation. The doll was placed in the foreground on the brick mantel as a symbolic feature of Anaïs's taste.

In reflecting on these impressions of Anaïs Nin as a *japonisante*, I will examine one Japanese literary woman's accomplishment as a token of appreciation for Nin's centenary birthday on February 21, 2003. I am confident that Anaïs Nin would have been pleased to know that Sumiko Yagawa appreciated her writings and sought to bring them to a wider audience.

Just as Nin felt the need to remove her Japanese doll from its glass case so that it could "breathe" naturally, her description of Nobuko in *Collages* seeking her independence from "centuries of confinement" is symbolized by the doll's traditional Japanese costume. Nin clearly hoped to create a liberated Japanese woman as her question in *In Favor of the Sensitive Man* gives evidence: "What kind of modern woman would emerge from the deep, masked, long-hidden Japanese woman of old?" (43) Nin also wanted to read more Japanese literature, much of which unfortunately had not been translated into English during her lifetime.

Tracing the genealogy of Anaïs Nin scholarship in Japan, a study such as *Anaïs Nin no Shôjo Jidai* (*Anaïs Nin as a Young Girl*) is rare. Yagawa, known chiefly as a translator of foreign literature for children[1] and as an essayist, wrote the book to help Japanese readers become familiar with Anaïs Nin. *Anaïs Nin as a Young Girl* was printed by a major Japanese publisher and was displayed by the most prestigious bookstores in Japan. The connection between Nin and Yagawa was rather unexpected for those who have read the works of one or the other, or for those in Japan who are familiar with the works of both. This essay will introduce *Anaïs Nin as a Young Girl* in terms of synthesizing Yagawa's exposition on the profiles of Nin's girlhood, and will highlight one aspect of contemporary trends of Nin study in Japan.

In the beginning of *Anaïs Nin as a Young Girl*, Yagawa explains why she became a devoted reader of Anaïs Nin. She confesses that she did not find Nin a particularly exciting writer when she first read the Japanese version of *Diary 1* (*Anaïs Nin no Nikki Dai Ikkan*) in the mid-1970s. Rather, Yagawa became an ardent reader of Nin after reading her unexpurgated diaries. After Yagawa read *Henry and June* and watched the movie of the same title, her curiosity about Nin's girlhood increased substantially. She began to wonder what extraordinary secrets might be hidden in Nin's youth and what her teenage years were like as well. What was it Nin had been yearning for since her adolescence? Yagawa states: "A nonprofessional judgment of investigating one's career accomplished after becoming an adult mostly offers clues to pin down what that particular woman 'wanted (missed)' in her teens." Yagawa reminds both herself and us that in the English language "want" means both *desire* and *deficiency*. From such double meanings, Yagawa refers to one of the common traits girls share: they tend to work hard to fulfill what they think they are "lacking (wanting)" when comparing themselves to other girls. Yagawa speculates, and feels she is not alone in her opinion, that the navigation of one's life is mostly determined by analyzing what is lacking (wanting) in one's individual existence after gaining consciousness to look at oneself and one's condition after the early teens.

As mentioned before, Yagawa did not write this book as a scholarly analysis, but rather to attract a more general Japanese readership. Yagawa presents a profile of Anaïs Nin as an adult before focusing on the essence of her book: what kind of young "girl" was Nin? Paralleling Yagawa's goals, Margot Beth Duxler indicates in *Seduction: A Portrait of Anaïs Nin*, "Rereading *Linotte* allowed me to work backward from the present to the past, picking up clues, evidence from the child about who the woman was to become" (15).

Amidst Yagawa's overall depiction of Nin's womanhood, what strikes her most is the relationship between Anaïs and Hugo (Hugh). Yagawa understands their matrimonial bond is only possible because of their utter sophistication and absolute confidence in each other's intellect and mind; otherwise there would have been no way to maintain their relationship. Yagawa sincerely admires such a reliable relationship. She speaks to us of her moments of admiration and her deep fascination with the couple as she viewed pictures of them performing a Flamenco dance in costume—a photo that appears in the fourth volume of *The Early Diary*. In fact, Yagawa thinks the book *Henry and June* actually should have been titled *Hugo and Anaïs*.

Here, of course, Yagawa indicates that the couple's encounter with Henry Miller seemed almost inevitable, and she sees the fatalistic meeting, if you will, and the subsequent relationship to be the seed of the personal rebirth that signifies both the awakening of Anaïs's sexuality and her craftsmanship as a writer. Yagawa points to Anaïs's life in the Paris of the 1930s as a period of rebirth and calls *Diary 1* an extraordinary book in its novelty and inquisitiveness. Yagawa sees this volume as Anaïs's autobiography rather than a diary as seen from the perspective of current readers who have read the series of the expurgated volumes. She calls the first volume a book of self-inspection and discusses her ironic views towards Nin's literary skills after she had spent decades trying to fictionalize it. Yagawa, given her seventy-one years of life, expresses her own sympathy and understanding of one writer's impatience at remaining a minor author when she is over sixty.

In addition to this profile of Anaïs Nin's womanhood, Yagawa also introduces Japanese readers to details of Nin's relationships with Hugo Guiler, Rupert Pole, and other men, including those surrounding her in Paris. Since Yagawa considers this period a renaissance for Nin, it allows her to develop an understanding of Nin's introspective character as she matured from childhood to greater levels of intellectual liberation throughout her life. It is this liberation that Yagawa celebrates in *Anaïs Nin as a Young Girl*. She sees Nin as a magnificent woman and wholeheartedly encourages new generations of girls to read her work. The preface helps Japanese readers understand some of Anaïs Nin's background as an adult and the social circles in which she moved as well as other influences in her life. Yagawa then focuses on developing a better understanding of Nin's childhood.

Yagawa's investigation spans Nin's youth from the time she was eleven years old until she was eighteen and met Hugo Guiler. She starts with excerpts from the first page of *Linotte*, dated July 25, 1914. She points to the hardship Nin experienced being exiled from Europe to the New World against the historical backdrop of the beginning of World War I as a life-shaping experience. She also praises the literary spirit demonstrated by young Anaïs's writing during the voyage to New York. Yagawa investigates her own motivation for exploring Nin's childhood and states that her image of Anaïs Nin was distinctively altered by reading *Linotte*. Her rising curiosity about the early years is spurred on the fact that Anaïs kept a continuous diary from the age of eleven. By being able to enter the personal realm of her diary, *Linotte*, Yagawa became more fascinated with Nin. She shares a memory of walking by a secondhand bookstall where *The Diary of Anne Frank* in Japanese was piled up among the others, almost imploring her to write about Nin's childhood diary for the benefit of her readers.

As for Yagawa, who accomplished much with notable translations of children's foreign and juvenile literature into Japanese, Nin's story of exile offers an excellent opportunity to delve deeply into her childhood because her daily life during this time was recorded faithfully. Yagawa astutely notes the lack of any father figure among the group of exiles with whom Nin associates and is interested in learning how she copes with this absence. Yagawa reminds the readers of the dramatic irony in which we are aware of a father and a daughter's reunion and the incidents of incest twenty years later.[2] Here, she wonders how much Anaïs was told of the fundamental causes of the exile based on her parent's divorce and by whom.

Leaving this important question for the reader to ponder, Yagawa examines *Linotte* chronologically. She declares that any girl over ten years of age has her own "history," and uses this as a point of reference in analyzing Anaïs, now eleven years old and looking back on her "history" in France and on her diary writing experience originally carried out in her mother tongue of French. In the New World, Anaïs was not an exception to the adverse experiences common to immigrants. The girl talks tête-à-tête to her diary-confidante not only of her exciting new life in New York but also of her sense of alienation as an immigrant. Yagawa introduces excerpts that mirror the young Nin's frustration and embarrassment as a non-native speaker in the classroom. I agree with Yagawa's focus on Anaïs's ESL syndrome, even though it was not as bad as the girl's case in Maxine Hong Kingston's *The Woman Warrior, Memoirs of a Girlhood Among Ghosts.* Still, Anaïs's linguistic shift from French to American English to exhibit her "brain" and "personality" in her classes must have been a difficult part of her adjustment.

Citing a September 13, 1914 letter from Anaïs's father, Yagawa examines Nin's separation from her father as she expected it to be— simply a temporary situation: Anaïs clings to her hope of returning to her "fatherland" where he lives, a hope she never completely abandons. She also reflects on the girl's faith in Catholicism that was cultivated in the Old World and believes it is this Catholic piety that gives Nin a way to mentally reconcile the distance between her and her father. Yagawa sees that the girl cannot obtain God, father, or France, save through her dreams, envisioning and praying that her mortal father metamorphoses into God in his absence. Yagawa also refers to Nin's *Winter of Artifice* and the description of the heroine: "Her true God was her father. At communion it was her father she received, and not God. She closed her eyes and swallowed the white bread with blissful tremors. She embraced her father in holy communion" (44).

Yagawa cites a January 19, 1915 diary entry because here she can find her father's future second wife Maria Luisa called by her rightful name instead of Maruca, the name Nin used in the years to follow. Yagawa believes that the sensitive Anaïs can certainly guess there is a love affair between her father and Maria Luisa as Nin notes in *Linotte*: "The other day I received a picture postcard of Mouleau from Maria Luisa. I asked Papa to thank her for me, but I confess to my diary that I don't like her. Isn't it she who has stolen my Papa from me? Yes, it is she, for she keeps him from coming to hold me in his arms and I shall never forgive her" (44). Yagawa also touches upon the story of Nin's "Stella" in *Winter of Artifice* in which the twelve-year-old Stella, upon her first meeting with Lora, the daughter of a wealthy family and her father's lover, whispers to her father to buy her new stockings. The meeting inspiring the scene in "Stella" apparently occurred when Nin was still in Europe and was therefore not written about in *Linotte*, but Yagawa highlights the obvious and unforgettable feelings of humiliation that resulted. Regarding the torn stockings, Yagawa reminds us of Anaïs's daily domestic chore to mend not only hers but also her younger brothers' socks when the family lived as immigrants in New York.

To her confidante, *Linotte*, Nin confesses that she still holds her "secrets," and that she cannot allow herself to tell all. Yagawa notes this tendency, especially in light of her parents' matrimonial discord, the loss of her father resulting in the "defeat" and exile of mother and daughter, and even worse, the women with whom her father consorts are not far removed in age from Anaïs herself. Yagawa understands Nin purposely staying away from unpleasant incidents and repressing any traumatic matters deep in her psyche. Nin does this so well that Yagawa believes that her perspective throughout *Linotte* is subjective. Yagawa even proffers that Nin's state of mind seems to almost mirror that of an autistic child.

It is only on November 7, 1919—five years after their immigration to New York—that Anaïs writes about the extent of her parents' marital problems in relating a conversation she had with her mother, recorded near the epilogue in *Linotte*. Yagawa's diction as a storyteller invites and entices Japanese readers to think about Anaïs's state of mind. To the girl's question, "Can Papa ever ask us to live with him?" her mother's reply is, "Oh, no, he has lost all his rights over you... Fifille, do you really think that one day Papa might come back and that we could be happy and all that? Those are romantic illusions, my daughter, which are good for nothing in life" (365). The sixteen-year-old Anaïs writes: "My childish illusions, the cherished dream of a reunion, the vision of a father in our home, the mysterious charm with which my imagination had surrounded the name 'Papa'—all that was in ruins, all that was dead. My romantic dream had become one of those real and terribly sad dramas such as we see all around us" (366). As one reads the diary, even with this shocking knowledge, Nin quickly tries to gather her self-resilience in face of this recognition of the end of her dream. Yagawa quotes many excerpts from this part of the girl's diary ending with Nin saying, "Oh! Let's not talk any more about the past. Only the future counts, and yet the Future is born of the Past... Courage! Courage!" (366).

Three years had passed since Nin's immigration to New York, and the spring of 1917 was literally a late spring's awakening for the indoor-orientated, fatherless fourteen-year-old girl whom Yagawa describes Nin to be. She points out two remarkable activities in Anaïs's pursuit of a career in arts: dancing in an amateur theatre group and modeling for a painter. Yagawa assumes that being a dancer and a model influenced Anaïs and her attempt to gain the self-confidence she needed to transcend her self-consciousness and to realize what it is like to have others pay attention to her.

Yagawa wonders why *Linotte* lacks any entries from January 1918 to March 1919 and laments that this prevents her from tracing the fifteen-year-old girl's emotional and physical transformation that would have been revealed in her adolescent writing.* Even so, given Anaïs's involvement in dance, Yagawa eagerly offers the belief that dancing was a bridge to early womanhood from childhood. Yagawa thinks Anaïs's Latin blood, rooted in her Cuban family heritage, allowed her to discover her talent in dancing. It is dancing that also brings the young Anaïs opportunities for courtship and ultimately leads to her engagement.

Along with her introduction of the sixteen-year-old girl's entries about her boyfriends and her growing social status, Yagawa could not help but digress to recall the dancing of Anaïs and Hugo after they had married. In 1921, Anaïs Nin met Hugh Parker Guiler and they married in 1923. According to Yagawa, both Anaïs and Hugo were the descendents of talented dancers and, as previously stated, she favors a particular picture of them dancing. She is struck not just by the couple as lovers, but also by the fact that they almost seem to relate to each other like psychological twins—a relationship that is described by Platon's theory of spherical body, at least, according to her. The snapshot of the couple dancing inspires Yagawa to emphasize the significant impact dancing had on Anaïs's life. The book ends with an idealized image of the marriage.

As for Anaïs's modeling attempts, Yagawa displays frustration that there are no satisfactory descriptions regarding this experience in *Linotte*. She attributes this deletion to Nin's reluctance to "tell all," using Rupert Pole's preface in *Henry and June* as evidence: "The puritanical Catholic girl who could not bring herself to describe to her diary her salacious (to her innocent mind) experiences as a model was now faced with recording her awakening to passions" (vii). Interestingly enough, Yagawa discusses Nin's 1940 erotic short story "A Model," which appears in *Little Birds*, and Anaïs Nin's period as a "madam of a literary salon" financially helping out poor writers in Paris. Yagawa translated "A Model" into Japanese herself and appends it with her exposition at the end of *Anaïs Nin as a Young Girl*. Yagawa warns readers not to confuse the story of "A Model" with what Anaïs could not confess to in the diary of her teens. She defends and praises Nin's lofty character as an artist and her woman's voice in her erotic writing, and declares her endless respect for Nin's notion of sexuality: the heightened sensuous quality of relations is only enhanced by the tie of love and sex in its emotional bondage (and not merely sex itself).

So, much of Anaïs's being a dancer and model embodies her transition from childhood to early adulthood. The last incident during her childhood, in terms of Yagawa's definition of it, has to do with

---

According to HBJ Editor John Ferrone, an entire volume had been lost.—Ed.

encountering her "knight," Hugo Guiler, and their marriage. She includes excerpts from February 7, 1921, two months before Anaïs met Hugo for the first time, one of which mentions Nin's acceptance to Columbia University. Yagawa points out the girl's desire for intellectual pursuit[3] as she writes in a letter to her cousin Eduardo: "Perhaps I do seem a featherhead and a 'fawn' whom it is a pity to startle and bewilder and bruise with cold philosophy. But I will show [the Columbia advisor] that the 'little French girl' (as she calls me) has gigantic ambitions, and that if people must smile at my *accent*, they will have to be serious when I write" (*Early Diary 2*, 146). Yagawa notes the Ariadne thread that winds through Anaïs and Hugo's encounter and inextricably intertwines them. It was fate that brought them together at the dance party where they first met and discovered their common interests. Hugo was a multi-talented man with a wonderful personality. He carried Emerson in his pocket and Stevenson was his favorite writer. He kept a diary, could recite Lamartine's poems, was a good dancer, and was financially mature enough to be employed at the National City Bank. He was also a student at Columbia University. Hugo was tall, trim, and five years older than Nin. With the amount of detail that Yagawa includes about him, it is evident that she thinks he is the perfect man for Anaïs to have married and that he filled the roles of both husband and father figure. She mentions Anaïs's concern for her mother's thoughts on her marriage, and theorizes that her decision to marry Hugo could have been an attempt to finally find a surrogate father. Yagawa, of course, shows that Hugo would be influential in Anaïs's life and help facilitate her career as a woman writer.

Sumiko Yagawa captures the essence of Anaïs Nin, the life she led and the possible reasons for the choices that she made in her life, as Duxler describes: "Who Anaïs was in *Linotte* was who she became" (104). Yagawa provides evidence for her assertion that Nin's life was shaped by her parents' divorce, her longing for her father, and her difficult immigration to New York. Nin worked through her experiences almost as if speaking a soliloquy publicly as she wrote in her journal on a consistent basis. As for some of her maturation processes, Yagawa takes educated guesses because even though Nin confided much in her journal, many significant aspects of her maturation are not recorded. Nonetheless, her genius comes through despite—and possibly because of—her childhood experiences. The end of her youth came when she met and married Hugo Guiler. This event also allowed Nin to overcome some of her early pain and gave her a basis from which she could excel in her creative endeavors as an adult.

In *Communion: the Female Search for Love,* bell hooks writes: "We wanted to be girls forever. As girls we felt we had power. We were strong and fierce and sure of ourselves. Somehow, as we made our entrance into the realm of young womanhood, we began to lose power. Research today confirms that young girls often feel strong, courageous, highly creative, and powerful until they begin to receive undermining sexist messages that encourage them to conform to conventional notions of femininity. To conform they have to give up power" (7). Some critics describe Sumiko Yagawa as a writer with a notion of being an eternal-girl. Although one may wonder whether Anaïs Nin wanted to be a girl forever, she was willing to become a woman, and moreover, she continuously searched to gain "power" throughout the stream of her life's-work of diary writing originating in her childhood. ❖

Notes

---

[1] Some of Sumiko Yagawa's (1931-2002) translations of foreign juvenile literature into Japanese are: *Little Women* by Louisa May Alcott, *Alice's Adventures in Wonderland* and *Through the Looking-Glass* by Lewis Carroll, *The Happy Prince* and *Lord Arthur Savile's Crime* by Oscar Wilde, *The Snow Goose* and *Snowflake* by Paul Gallico, and *Juggler's Tale* by Michael Ende.

[2] Sumiko Yagawa published *Chichi no Musumetachi—Mari Mori to Anaïs Nin (Father's daughter—Mari Mori and Anaïs Nin)* in 1997. Yagawa renders the comparisons between Ougai Mori (1863-1911), translator of *Faust* and a naval surgeon's daughter that was one of the notable Japanese writers in the Meiji period, Mari Mori (1903-1987), a Japanese woman writer and essayist, and Anaïs Nin in terms of their father-daughter relationships. Yagawa thinks if Mari's father complex is a positive one, then that of Anaïs is a negative one. Yagawa believes one pattern of incest is namely a father's girl's first step in the process to her own self-establishment.

[3] Yagawa uses a metaphor of the Queen's mirror in *Snow White* for young Anaïs's diary. As for Anaïs, unlike the Queen's desire for the affirmation of beauty ("You are the fairest one of all"), she wants both beauty *and* intelligence and to be reassured that "You are the wisest one of all." Cf. *Chichi no Musumetachi—Mari Mori to Anaïs Nin (Father's daughter—Mari Mori and Anaïs Nin)*, Shinchosh, 1997, p. 102. Duxler also refers to the metaphor of mirrors: "The themes of being understood that first appear in *Linotte,* are sometimes expressed by the image of a mirror as a reflection of the self—a metaphor that fascinated Anaïs throughout her life" (141).

Claudine Brelet

Villa Seurat and Parc Montsouris
Fragments of a rich past

illa Seurat and Parc Montsouris are two inseparable remnants of a Paris that existed long ago, the Paris of the artists living between the two great wars, who were known as the "*Montparnos*." The Montparnos' territory extended from Gare Montparnasse to Pont Royal, from where blvd St-Michel and rue St-Jacques end, to Parc Montsouris. As recently as the 1960s, the joyous, undulating ambiance that brought to life a timeless *décor* found in such famous cafés-brasseries as La Coupole, La Dôme, Le Sélect, La Rotonde, and La Closerie des Lilas, hardly seemed different than that familiar to Anaïs Nin, Henry Miller, and Lawrence Durrell before the outbreak of World War II.

Indeed, a more or less conscious and sometimes even fluid continuity existed between the two generations that had at one time or another frequented these establishments, or who had lived in or near the Montparnasse Quarter. It was still possible to traverse Paris at any hour and say that it was "the only city in the world where one can be happy with nothing," as Miller once did.

However, with the death of André Breton in 1966, and then the desecration of the cobblestone streets by the tar machines after the Latin Quarter student demonstrations of 1968, Paris would never be the same again. Soon, like wildfire, well-to-do tourists and visitors sprouting from the *autobuses* supplanted the artists, students, and intellectuals, ironically destroying the very atmosphere they were seeking. With the influx of tourism, the price of a simple *café-noir* soon reached what used to be the price of a full meal, driving away the remaining inhabitants of the quarter.

Up until 1844, the southern boundary of Paris ended with blvd St-Jacques and was marked by the walls of the *Fermiers Généraux.** This space, which belonged to the pastoral community of Gentilly, became what is now the 14th arrondissement of Paris, otherwise known as Montparnasse.

The construction of the Montsouris reservoir, one of Paris's seven reservoirs, was begun by famed Parisian architect Haussmann in 1858

Paris was surrounded by a 15 foot wall built in 1784 for the purpose of facilitating the taxation of goods entering the city.—Ed.

and completed in 1874, above the ancient quarries from which the stone used to build Paris had been mined. Its summit, covered with an immense lawn, crowns an "invisible cathedral" whose arches, rooted in the subterranean mines, evoke the mystery of the cisterns of Alexandria. Known as a *département de l'eau*, the reservoir houses the arrival of waters from the Marne, the Seine, and the Loing, which flows through the marshes, prairies, and thick forests of Fontainebleau. It also receives the waters of the Bièvre,[*] which is now totally covered and re-channeled. Water is at the heart of Montparnasse, and to this day has its devotees who worship it in a cult-like fashion. Perched atop the lawns of the reservoir are what appear to be "glass cathedrals," but are in fact buildings in which the controls of the reservoir are found.

Detail of bakery window

The 16-hectare Parc Montsouris, conceived by the celebrated landscape designer Jean-Charles Alphand (who also designed Parc Monceau near l'Étoile, and that of the Buttes Chaumont on the eastern side of Paris), was built much like the reservoir—above the quarries with an artificial lake. Before becoming one of the three most beautiful parks in Paris, Montsouris was given the nickname "*Moque-Souris*" because in ancient times the area's windmills were haunted by mice (*souris*), and the wheat flour brought from neighboring Beauce was reduced greatly in size by their need for nourishment.

Like the ancient cults, the water cult of the quarter has had its sacrifices: having just been filled with water, the lake of Parc Montsouris suddenly emptied itself into the chasms below during the park's inauguration in 1869, prompting the suicide of the engineer in charge. But, by the grace of a beautiful music gazebo built near the southern edge of the lake, at the foot of cascading water, the memory of this drama soon faded with the musical strains of Offenbach. A half-century later, during the years when Nin and Miller frequented the area,

---

[*]*This river's name has ancient Gallic origins in the European* castor, *known in Flemish as the* bever, *in German as the* beber, *and in English the* beaver.

his lively and popular music was sometimes replaced by the aesthetics of modern music, minimalist and occasionally jazzy. This trend was begun by one of the "rascals" of the Conservatoire, Erik Satie, who influenced the great composers of the time: Ravel, Debussy, Stravinsky, Milhaud, Fauré…

Parc Montsouris

This curved park, a vast space of freedom, has maintained a sense of eternity, perhaps due to the presence of a somewhat inexpressible *autre monde*, as the Celts and Gauls called it, a world where water symbolizing rebirth mingles with the sleep of the dead. Millions of skeletons are arranged in haphazard patterns in the galleries of the catacombs, a vast underground labyrinth occupying a hundred square kilometers of the abandoned mines in Montparnasse, extending to the depths beneath Parc Montsouris, sometimes in several superimposed levels. The catacombs are next to the "temple of water," the Montsouris Reservoir, and are very humid, dark, and dank. It is easy to get lost in the silence and the opacity of the centuries while a few dozen meters above the traffic of Place Denfert-Rochereau roars. The neighborhood *gamins* play some of their perilous adventure games in this seemingly endless maze.

Beginning with the Exposition Universale of 1889, followed by a retrospective of Gaugin's work in 1903, and that of Cézanne in 1907, the quiet quarter inhabited by artisans and small garden-markets began wooing the most influential artists of the time. Like the honey of the flowers of its gardens, it attracted from the butte of Montmartre the likes of Gauguin, Rousseau, Matisse, Picasso, as well as writers Apollinaire and Cendrars, among many others. To facilitate this mass migration, the North-South Métro line (Montmartre-Montparnasse) was established, and blvd Raspail opened in 1910.

During the time between the two wars, the district continued changing. Certainly, here and there, some of the buildings designed by Haussmann were already dressed in new, rich-looking carved stone façades in a manner considered insolent in this still rustic quarter. Perhaps the most spectacular construction was that of an ensemble of ateliers and apartments from 1924 to 1926 on a paved dead-end street christened Villa Seurat, one of the many *villas* bordered by small but stately houses that were becoming fashionable in Paris. Combining modernism with the natural presence of what was (and still is) the greenest district in Paris, architect André Lurçat designed eight of the residences that line Villa Seurat, one of which was for his brother Jean, an artist known for his blazing tapestries. These structures were soon accompanied by others, including one designed by the Perret brothers for Russian sculptor Chana Orloff. With their overhanging rooftop terraces, brightly colored façades, and large picture windows, these buildings were actual living quarters as well as ateliers for the artists.

Very close to Montparnasse and Parc Montsouris, and surrounded by craftsmen, florists, butchers, plumbers, and shopkeepers, a shop on a corner of Villa Seurat became a center where children came to learn the techniques of shaping clay and the strokes of the brush. This peaceful impasse situated on an ever-narrowing hallowed terrain, squeezed by an ever-expanding city, is a reminder of an artistic part of Paris, a legendary district steeped in the reverence of water and nature. Small gardens hide at the end of passages often inaccessible to those without the keys to the buildings shrouding them. The result of Lurçat's achievement in Villa Seurat maintains even today a bit of urbane humanity in the midst of a city in a constant state of flux.

Nothing seems to have changed since the days of "art for art's sake" and literature "to fix the blood and tripe of the time," as Miller said. The houses on rue Georges Braque (where the painter made his fortune) appear to ignore the outside world that has crept in…they are aged like those hunched with the pain of arthritis, lost on meandering and chaotic alleyways, hidden as though avoiding the curious. There, the cars are suddenly very modest and all small, mostly hatchbacks and mini-cars. The quarter is filled with families. Some of the old guard say the current state of affairs is sad, especially on Sunday when the bars and small shops with names such as *La Maison de l'Escargot* and *Les Caves de Bacchus*, once known to the trio of Nin, Miller, and Durrell, are closed.

It was at No. 18 Villa Seurat, the house of American writer Michael Fraenkel, where Henry Miller began the first of several works that he would become famous for, *Tropic of Cancer*, published in 1934 by Obelisk Press. Would this work have been achieved at all had it not been for the benevolence of Anaïs Nin, who "kept" Miller in this divine and occult, wet and green underbelly of an eternal Paris?

No. 18 Villa Seurat

Years later, during a second stay at the same address, Miller began a correspondence with the astrologist Dane Rudhyar. Of this, he later noted that Rudhyar had a special gift of being able to present a mental picture of the totality of his subject, to induce a sense of the profound spiritual significance of the relationship between all things. It seems very likely that Miller recognized the "spirit of the place" during the Villa Seurat years.

Villa Seurat faces rue Tombe-Issoire, which borders the Montsouris Reservoir. Illuminated at night, the glass houses atop the reservoir take on fairytale-like forms, adding a permanent festive atmosphere to this quiet and peaceful neighborhood, sometimes brightened by the laughter of bands of students returning to the Latin Quarter from the *Cité Internationale Universitaire*. One imagines that their laughter, fusing with summer nights along avenue Reille, resounds in the echoes of that of Miller and Durrell, who may have been returning from an escapade at the Coupole. One imagines the two of them stopping off at Villa Seurat, perhaps, and then proceeding on their way to Durrell's lodgings in a small three-story building, skirting Parc Montsouris and passing over the tracks of the train that took commuters back and forth between Paris and the suburbs.

At the end of the 1960s, La Coupole was still the nighttime headquarters of Lawrence Durrell. He would meet his friends there each time he came to Paris, descending from a hotel close to the Vavin Métro, kitty-corner from blvd Raspail, facing rue de la Grande Chaumière. Thanks to him, I rediscovered the charm of Parc

Montsouris during a pilgrimage to Villa Seurat. We went one day to visit his friend Alexandre Bloch, a UNESCO translator, who is also a poet and novelist writing under the name Jean Blot. We met him at his house in what is known as the Cité Florale (the site of a pond up until the 19th Century), where the streets take the names of flowers: *des Glycines, des Iris, des Volubilis*. From there we visited another of Durrell's friends in a rare atelier that had survived the modernization of avenue René Coty—that of the photographer Brassaï, whose intense gaze I shall never forget, that camera-eye of his, very black and very similar to that of his friend Picasso.

Yes, everything is a part of something else, Rudhyar said, a view shared by my great-uncle, Charles Chéneveau. He was a student of Becquerel, then professor at the Sorbonne and the Institute of Physics and Chemistry in Paris, and lived in Montparnasse, said today to be the home of "superior intellectual professionals." (They constitute more than 26% of the population of the 14th arrondissement compared to a little more than 4% artisans and shopkeepers—hardly practical in the daily lives of the inhabitants.) My uncle lived during the era of scientific pioneering, having himself created new paradigms, including inventing the electromagnetic balance with Pierre Curie.

Lawrence Durrell's lodgings

"*Le hasard n'existe pas*," André Breton was fond of saying to anyone who would listen. Perhaps this applies to the lives of Miller and especially Durrell, who, in his way, impacted my life as much as Miller impacted his. Years later, on the eve of 2000, my youngest daughter Valentine (nicknamed Val) lived 200 meters from Villa Seurat. Nothing there had changed. Not the paved alleyways, nor the hieratic temple of water in the Montsouris Reservoir. Not the curious surveyor's marker located on the southern end of Paris and the meridian[*] of Paris, which two centuries ago made it possible for the *Observatoire* to be placed correctly (and *"par hasard"* the other marker is hidden in a house in Montmartre). Not even the restaurant formerly named *Le Jardin de la Paresse* (Garden of Idleness), a pavilion in the *Belle Epoque* style, where one can still enjoy the subtleties of the best classic French cuisine, for example, *râble de lièvre servi rosé à la châtelaine* or the *macaron moelleux aux framboises...* Even the urbanization taking place on ground cleared by the destruction of old ateliers by the transportation authority of Paris (not without protest from the "natives" of Montsouris) is almost forgiven since it has permitted the discovery of two ancient aqueducts (one from the 2nd Century, Gallo-Roman, and the other from 1613, commissioned by Marie de Médicis to bring drinkable water to the Luxembourg Palace). Today, a "crypt" has been built to protect and publicly display a portion of the Gallo-Roman aqueduct to remind Parisians of the time when Paris was called by its Roman name, "Lutecia."

Montparnasse was *une ville initiatique*, if there ever was one for Miller and Nin, one with an Alexandrian flavor for Durrell. It is through their fictional characters—enchanted with the mystical voluptuousness of their surroundings—that they reveal the history, magic, and poetry of the France of Villon, Rabelais, and Baudelaire, the France of true poets in love with eternal freedom. ❖

—Translated from the French by Paul Herron

Detail of house on Villa Seurat

---

[*]*On June 21, 1667, the summer solstice, the meridian of Paris was mapped and was used for not only the location of the observatory, but also as the reference median for all of France.—Ed.*

Diane Allerdyce

Photograph
For Sharon Spencer

New Year's Day, 2003

Today I have been thinking a lot of disappointment
of honor and friendship,
of silk scarves and your own soft eyes.

In the photograph above my computer
on the desk that recently came back to me when John
moved into a furnished apartment and gave me everything
that used to be mine before we divorced,
you and I smile outward.

I found the photo again when I moved out
of my university office last summer
and placed it on the desk at home.

In this picture, you are turbaned and well.
You're wearing long beads, and I
am wearing your arm like a favorite shawl.

We were in Cincinnati at a conference where people like us
share common dreams,
the stuff we were made on.
My book about Anaïs lies on the table before us.

You and Paul and Rochelle and I noticed
how the Miller scholars and the Durrells gathered in the room where
    refreshments were served
while those there to talk about Nin were assigned an adjacent space.
It was a minor letdown.

Paul and I discussed the meaning of the phrase "minor writer."
As in the music of the womb, as in "minor key."
It was something to celebrate, and honor.
So we all ordered coffee in the shop and wore red to the sessions.
You defended a valiant point passionately during the
    questions and answers.

Later you told me about your own part of New Jersey.

Day after day lately, I re-read your books, stare at the photo of you on the
    back cover
of *Collage of Dreams*,
the one where you could easily be mistaken for Anaïs.

My thoughts dance around and around
the news of your losing Montclair, the email from Paul
that you and Gunther were gone.

And today,
all day,
I've been thinking a lot about disappointment,
about how it is our teacher, our muse,
how we can still make beauty out of what is stillborn.

The wooden floors shift beneath my bare feet.
I shall emerge from the ether one of these days; I can feel it.

It is your kindness I remember most. ❖

---

*Talk with Sharon over the telephone: She laughs like a school-
girl—almost exaggeratedly feminine before I sent her to Bogner,
playing at schoolgirl rather than brilliant scholar and teacher. Her
book is dazzling. Now she tells me she finds it hard to accept her
maturity.*
    *She and I repudiate the homely role of liberated women. She
dresses exquisitely. In fact she is the only woman to wear a dress I
hungered for. She loaned it to me... She has a delicate face, big eyes,
finely designed features, a delicate long neck. Her expression is
seductive, lively, playful. She is slender. Her voice is light. (Diary 7,
300)*

Yuko Yaguchi

Twittering Machine of Paradise
Glimpses of two of Anaïs Nin's Japanese daughters

On May 29, 2002, a well-known Japanese woman of letters, Sumiko Yagawa, committed suicide at the age of seventy-one. The next day, on May 30, her new book entitled *Anaïs Nin as a Young Girl*, in which she introduces excerpts of *Linotte* in excellent translation and offers her unique view on "being a girl," was published, seemingly her last will and testament.

It was also in the spring seven years before, on April 21, 1995, that another Japanese woman writer who played an inerasable role in Nin's reception in Japan passed away from a ruptured artery at the age of fifty-six. Masako Meio was then studying at the Steiner College in Fair Oaks, California. Though her death was natural, it was so sudden and shocking that some felt it was almost like a suicide.[1]

The two women had more than a few things in common. Apart from being two of the best Japanese translators of Anaïs Nin and themselves writers of unique talents, at least one from each set of parents was a teacher, both were exceptionally proficient in foreign language(s) for Japanese of their generation, and they were both married to men of letters, name, and authority. On the other hand, there were marked contrasts between them, most notably their differing viewpoints on Anaïs Nin, which create a multi-faceted portrait of Nin when read as a palimpsest.

Since Yagawa often mentions that Anaïs was born in the same year as her mother, and Meio once wrote an essay titled "The Daughters of Anaïs Nin,"[2] they may be rightfully considered two of Nin's Japanese daughters. How did Anaïs Nin influence and inspire these two daughters from the Far East who were to die such tragic deaths?

Masako Meio—A Woman with Four Names

I was introduced to the world of Anaïs Nin through Masako Hara's Japanese translation of *The Diary of Anaïs Nin Volume 1*. Not only is the translation written as if Anaïs herself is speaking directly to us, the "Translator's Afterword" is, in my opinion, one of the best essays ever written on Anaïs Nin, not only in Japanese but also in English. Hara's insight stands apart from the stereotypical worship/accusatory responses to Nin, and is filled with critical sympathy of a woman sharing the same intellectual/artistic/life stage with the author (the translator was then in her early thirties, about the same age as the diarist in the volume).

As early as 1974, Hara declared Anaïs Nin's *Diary* a grand fiction, that Nin's obsessive search for "true self" itself betrays its absence—to Anaïs Nin womanhood is more of an "idea" than "nature," which sounds too postmodern to have been said in the seventies.

Though I came to know her as Masako Hara, she later wrote novels by the name of Masako Meio. In 1979 Meio made a literary debut with *A Glimpse of a Woman*, which earned her the prominent Bungei Literary Award. She also used the name Masako Karatani after marriage, as a critic and translator. When the Japanese translation of *Diary 1* was published as a paperback edition in 1991, the translator procured herself a fourth name, Akie Hara. While Anaïs Nin declared possession of a "thousand faces," Meio literally lived her life with four names, suggesting multiplicity/fragmentation of identity, a familiar theme to Nin readers.

Judith Butler, in discussing Willa Cather's crossing of gender/sexuality, makes a noteworthy point which could explain Meio's obsession with names as well as indicate her literary theme:

> For women, then, propriety is achieved through having a changeable name through the exchange of names, which means that the name is never permanent, and that the identity secured through the name is always dependent on the social exigencies of paternity and marriage. Expropriation is thus the condition of identity for women. Identity is secured precisely in and through the transfer of the name, the name as a site of transfer or substitution, the name, then, as precisely what is always impermanent, different from itself, more than itself, the non-self-identical.[3]

Here Butler counterplots a social code which is supposed to interfere with women's independence/identity in the name of propriety, and transfers it in the postmodern context. Yet as it is manifest in Butler's discussion, woman's changeable name works as a revolving door of the modern/postmodern; while it restricts women's identity within the bounds of paternity and marriage, it paradoxically enables women to escape the clutching hands of the Father.

Meio's female character is driven by a double-edged fear of, and desire for, multiple identity. Yukiko, in Meio's autobiographical novel *A Glimpse of a Woman*, confesses that she gets bored with herself before anyone gets bored with her and lives a "self which is scarcely born before ruptured like an unfinished book."[4] She always dreams of another self she could have lived if she hadn't chosen this life. She is obsessed with a Puerto Rican "Dark Lady," Dolores, a femme fatale who torments her husband Leonard, an Anglo-Saxon Shakespearean. Yukiko-Leonard-Dolores form a triangle in the manner of Anaïs-Henry-June. Yukiko identifies herself sometimes with Dolores, sometimes with Leonard, and has an ambivalent desire to tear up and make up their relationship.

The difference lies outside the triangle: while Anaïs was married to the "generous" Hugo, Yukiko's husband, a visiting scholar to a university in New Haven, serves as a criterion for Yukiko to assume value (O paternity!). Her father was also the indignant God, the "rigid law rather than a human father"[5] (the law of the Father!). When the severe, often violent father softens once in a while, she feels so nervous it almost takes on an erotic air. Yukiko is afraid she might be taking her revenge on her children when she scolds or beats them hard. Later it is revealed that the exotic Dark Lady Dolores is also under control and subjected to the violence of her scholar husband, a "big man" from the United States, the symbol of power and authority.

Noriko Mizuta, a pioneering feminist critic in Japan, insightfully points out that Yukiko and Dolores, who are seemingly in direct contrast with one another, are actually two domestic women, both within the domain of patriarchy, and that the narrative of modern women cannot escape the modern family which produced the women themselves.

Alongside the father-daughter narrative in the modern family romance is romantic love ideology, or what another prominent Japanese feminist, Chizuko Ueno, calls the "couple illusion,"[6] which is definitely detectable in Meio's novels.

In the "Translator's Afterword" in the paperback edition of the *Diary 1*, Meio recollects that women of her generation looked up to Sartre and Beauvoir as the ideal couple and were busy looking for *their* Sartre. She adds, to her regret, that after Beauvoir's death, it was revealed that instead of being the supposed role model who sought gender equality to the hilt, she was actually subjugated to her great partner ideologically and sexually, serving as mother in order not to lose him.

This could be read as the self-criticism that put an end to Meio's twenty-year marriage to Kojin Karatani, "arguably the most influential critic in Japan in the past twenty years,"[7] presumably when she was writing her last novel, *The Son of the Southern Cross*. In the posthumously published novel—the last of her autobiographical family narratives and most likely a metaphorical "will"—we find harsh criticism of Japanese marriage, in which a woman is doomed to play the role of mother to her husband, who is under the spell and control of his birth mother. Meio's character Mioko laments falling into the trap that is Japan, entrapping herself in marriage. Her architect husband Iwao serves on one hand as a tyrant-father who captures Mioko's soul by fear and is incapable of loving his sons, on the other as a spoiled child who declares that his doing housework is a national waste (!)

The feminist historian Etsuko Yamashita reports that she received through an editor Meio's unpublished English essay "Glimpses of the Present-Day Japanese Women" in 1992, in which Meio refers to *Southern Cross* as the epitome of her forty-six years as a woman deeply influenced by the West.[8] Meio, as Yamashita tells us, calls the behavior pattern of her generation for Japanese women trapped in the role of the Great Mother archetype a "general hushing,"[9] and points to Anaïs Nin, who declared she would "write as a woman," as a role model of the future generation. Meio's prediction may come true if we remember that Anaïs Nin continued "shedding yesterday's woman to pursue a new vision,"[10] and that the word "woman" itself, according to Butler, is a "term in process, a becoming, a construction that cannot rightfully be said to originate or to end."[11]

Meio defines Anaïs Nin as "a winner, a strong woman and a woman with celestial wings."[12] It is true that Anaïs refused to be

Masako Meio

dominated by one man, that she was determined not to be like her mother, as is often the case with modern woman writers. She didn't deny motherhood totally but rather chose to be a symbolic one. Kate Millet once called Anaïs a "Mother to Us All,"[13]—she was a mother not only to men and art, as is sometimes (mis)understood, but also to women who welcomed the publication of the *Diary*, saying Anaïs wrote *their* diary. It is to transgress or subvert women's dual stereotypes if the pleasure-seeking woman is also a "Mother to Us All," creating another woman, Dona Juana-Mary-Anaïs. Nevertheless and imaginably, it requires a woman with idiosyncratic ability and ambition to achieve that state, who is free from a "fear of flying" and is determined to devote her life to an aerial effort. In

Children of the Albatross Anaïs Nin has a research scientist explain with how much intensity birds live their lives:

> Their body temperatures are regularly as high as 105 to 110 degrees, and anyone who has watched a bird at close range must have seen how its whole body vibrates with the furious pounding of its pulse… The bird's indrawn breath not only fills its lungs, but also passes on through myriads of tiny tubules into air sacs that fill every space in the bird's body not occupied by vital organs. Furthermore the air sacs connect with many of the birds' bones, which are not filled with marrow as animals' bones are, but are hollow. These reserve air tanks provide fuel for the bird's intensive life, and at the same time add to its buoyancy in flight.[14]

For a human being to realize the state of a bird would mean strenuous, perhaps almost inhuman will and energy. The extent of freedom Anaïs Nin acquired herself was equal to the depth of her inner darkness and secrecy. This inaccessibility to Nin's core of truth more than a quarter of a century after her death and a century after her birth might partially explain why she remains in the ambiguous or peripheral realm as a writer. Anaïs Nin's greatest secret, in any case, is how she could escape insanity (unlike Zelda Fitzgerald or Chieko Takamura[15]), or suicide (unlike Sylvia Plath or Sumiko Yagawa), and transform herself into a "woman with celestial wings."

Meio's female character, however energetic, talented and ambitious, often stumbles before her husband's judgmental statements and suffers in silence. But the writer refused to be a hushed wife by representing herself in the novels, in a way simultaneously playing the roles of Anaïs Nin and Nancy Durrell as described in *Diary 2*: "'Shut up,' says Larry to Nancy. She looks at me strangely, as if expecting me to defend her, explain her. Nancy, I won't shut up. I have a great deal to say, for June, for you, for other women."[16]

One feels at a loss whether to call it tragic or inspirational, but Meio, as a writer, survived the wife who may have sacrificed her life in the "trap that is Japan," and left her works to younger daughters of Anaïs Nin and of Masako Meio herself.

Sumiko Yagawa: The Immortal Anti-Girl

While Meio's interest in Anaïs Nin is focused on Nin as woman/writer, her desire for maturity, and all the difficulties she experiences, Sumiko Yagawa makes it clear that her fascination with

Nin comes mostly from the unexpurgated diary of her younger days, *Linotte*. In *Anaïs Nin as a Young Girl*, Yagawa introduces in superb translation the young Anaïs or "Linotte" ("little bird," a nickname given by her mother) who seems charming and lovable to Japanese readers, while accurately indicating that the volume of *Linotte* lacks description between January 8, 1918 and March 1919[*] and that the young Anaïs restrains herself from writing anything physical or sexual so that we don't even know when she had her first menstruation.

Yagawa names Anaïs Nin and Anne Frank as the two true authors of literature written by and for children. The young Anaïs is referred to as the "eldest daughter in a fatherless family" or the "unpopular immigrant girl," quite different from the image of Anaïs as a young woman rich in love and talent, but akin to Yagawa's definition of the "anti-girl." She expounds that the anti-girl is a girl who cannot get along with herself and the world, someone like Anaïs/Sumiko who believes she is ugly and escapes into the "wordland."[17] She also adds that in order to immortalize a girl, which is only a phase in process (interestingly in accordance with Butler's interpretation of woman), one should crown her with a word of negation such as "anti," "no," "non," and that a girl who doesn't say *no* is no girl.

In other words, Yagawa's anti-girl, which in her definition has nothing to do with age, is someone who cannot be content with female gender. Any woman writer will keep this anti-girl in an inner room of her own, as Yagawa herself (again self-mockingly?) labels a woman writer an unhappy outcome of the anti-girl. In the same context, Noriko Mizuta says that the girl as archetype/double plays a crucial role for modern woman writers.[18] The archetypal girl, such as Alice or Princess Kaguya in a Japanese fairytale, belongs nowhere in this world and therefore functions as a messenger, just

Sumiko Yagawa

as a woman writer occupying a peripheral place in society speaks as a medium.

Another important concept Yagawa adopts is that of a Jungian "father's daughter." In *Father's Daughters: Mari Mori and Anaïs Nin*, published five years before *Anaïs Nin as a Young Girl*, she takes up two woman writers, one from Japan and the other from America, as examples of a father's daughter who identifies more with father than mother. Yagawa assumes that any girl residing in the "wordland" whose best friend is a book or a father's daughter, which corresponds to the feminist idea that written words are basically male property and tradition, that the oral is female.

She regards Anaïs Nin a proficient bilingual who speaks men's and women's languages, pointing to *Henry and June* in which Anaïs serves as a translator between the two. (We can trace the translator Anaïs in *Linotte*, in which she tries to reconcile the separated parents.) Yagawa herself remembers having two accents in her family: her father's accent from a southern part of Japan and her mother's Tokyo accent which is considered to be standard Japanese. Her father was a scholar of English literature whose books nourished her mind, and her mother was a "spoiled" housewife who was the anti-girl's anti-mentor, so to speak. Nevertheless, Yagawa later found her "mother tongue," a smooth Tokyo accent she inherited from her mother, a great help when she translated children's books. She became a professional translator (from English, French and German into Japanese) as a means of livelihood after divorce, and her rule was to translate books out of which she heard her own Japanese while reading them.

Yagawa portrays the "little bird" Anaïs as someone who loves her hard-working mother, respects her absent musician father, and is devoted to both, who gradually finds out she is not ugly as told by her father, and finally finds her true love in Hugo Guiler. The book ends rather abruptly in a naïve idealization of the Anaïs-Hugo marriage, concluding that Anaïs finally finds her lost father in young Hugo.

The ending feels not only abrupt, but also unfinished since we know that their marriage (including its sexuality, about which Yagawa admits Anaïs was self-repressive until her encounter with Henry Miller) strayed far from any happy conclusion. Yagawa's ending is almost like a fairytale ending in which a poor, young girl is rescued by a handsome prince. It is perhaps more intriguing than persuasive as to why she ended her book that way.

Yagawa admires the Anaïs-Hugo relationship ("This mutual trust!"[19]) and compares it to a pair of identical twins or a Platonic union of androgynous halves. We find the almost identical description in her autobiographical fantasy *A Woman Called Rabbit*, written "like automatic writing" six months after a divorce from Tatsuhiko Shibusawa, a cult critic of French literature, whose Japanese translations of Marquis de Sade resulted in obscenity charges. In Yagawa's *Rabbit*, dedicated "To Him," the narrator recollects her failed marriage: "We were an ideal couple, the 'one and only' match, as they said and we believed, for we were opposites. He had everything I lacked, and vice versa. We were one, yes, we were doubles." A listener replies, "It's Platonic. I envy you, having met your double."

In such an ideal marriage as the narrator describes it, "He was literally my master, for me to obey. If he was to be called 'husband,' I should be 'wife.'" Calling one's husband "master" may appear an anachronism in English, yet (believe it or not) it is a common practice in present-day Japan. Though some may say it is only nominal, in 1983 Yagawa wrote, in a form of autobiographical fiction, that it was literally the case in her marriage. More shockingly and/or metaphorically telling is the husband's remark "Woman is not human," to which the wife responds, "You are right."

> If woman is not human, she is inhuman. God. A thing. A beast. Whatever... What am I? ...
> If he is man, I am woman.
> If he is an animal, I am an angel.
> If he is human, am I a human figure? ...
> However / If he is a child, I am his mother.[20]

We should remind ourselves that in English as well, we let "man" represent human beings until only several decades ago. Therefore, Shibusawa's and Yagawa's master-servant relationship, in which the servant testifies she was busy and content with being the master's wife-mother-secretary-housekeeper, cannot be regarded as a backward example in the Far East, but as portraying a universal phenomenon concerning gender.

The first chapter of *Rabbit* is titled "The Wing." The "wing" is a strange little bone-like thing in the shape of a "V." The narrator converses with a man about it as follows:

> "It's so delicate... I bet it must be the wing of an angel figure or something."
> "Yes, a figure, and an angel... By implanting this plastic wing inside my body, I could transform into an angel both in name and reality. Into a fake angel flying empty-heartedly upon the air, against nature, feet over the ground, with artificial wings."[21]

The wing that transfigures a woman into a fake angel is an intrauterine device, an IUD. The narrator discloses that in order to live up to her husband's principle to not seek everyone's happiness, she had to abort burgeoning lives that came to her as they did to everyone else, and that her husband gave her the "plastic wing" so he can monopolize her as mother. This is how she became, in the double meaning of the word, an "ideal" mother embracing a fake child-husband, who is inseparably embraced by his biological mother—exactly the same portrait of marriage as Meio depicted.

According to an essay Yagawa wrote three months before her death, she had to go through a series of abortions during the nearly two decade marriage to Shibusawa: "Now I think about it, it was always the wife who had to bleed for the no-child principle. There was a time I almost uttered, 'Is it not unfair?' But it was never voiced in the end."[22] When she broke the silence, it was the end of their Platonic union and his paradise.

For Yagawa, the "plastic wing" was also the killer of possible lives. If we remember once again Anaïs Nin's vivid description of a bird's aerial mechanism which is fueled with its own will to fly, Yagawa's angel feels more like a kite or a puppet manipulated by her lord and master. Likewise, while Nin is a survivor of an abortion made of her own will, as detailed in *Incest*, Yagawa is rather a victim of the abortions, carried out according to her husband's phallo-egocentric principle, which may well be labeled another form of domestic violence.

To speak, or not to speak; that is Yagawa's question.

In *The Lost Garden*, which can be regarded as a retelling of *Rabbit*, the narrator FG analyzes the monstrosity she has directed at her ex-husband. She concludes that it does not lie in her final betrayal, but rather in the utmost obedience with which she never said *no* in a decade of marriage, something she regrets. Bearing in mind the "Author's Note" to *The Immortal Girl*, which concludes that a girl who says *no* is no girl, Yagawa's life passage was that of anti-Bildungsroman, in which the anti-girl married to be an obedient wife, then divorced to be the immortal girl (again).

In the coda of *Garden*, FG explains the failure of her marriage to EH and feels frustrated:

> No. This man doesn't understand, either. Do you know what I really want to say? More. There's a lot more to it...
> Vain. All is vain without words.
> FG swallows all those unvoiced words and uttered instead:
> "All I want to say is—let me be silent. Period."[23]

The predictive passage makes us wonder if silence was Yagawa's last word. There is a claim that she was to meet an editor to work on a magazine's special edition featuring Nin[24] several days after her death, which tempts us to think her suicide was impulsive. On the other hand, some facts—a day's difference between her death and the publication of *Anaïs Nin as a Young Girl*, that she sent the book to many of her friends as if in time for her own death, and that her favorite music was playing by her body—speak otherwise.

In the previously mentioned essay written three months before her death, Yagawa acknowledges that her aim as a writer is to "speak out of experience written in my body as text."[25] Could we go a step further and hypothesize that she aimed to speak through her (dead) body, turning it into her final work of art, as suggested by the original title of *Rabbit*, "The Confession of a Beautiful (Dead) Body"? If that is the case, Yagawa transcends Nin's ambition of creating her life as art and reaches out to break the boundary between life and death, in the same manner as Gayatri Spivak interprets/translates an Indian woman's suicide: "Bhubaneswari attempted to 'speak' by turning her body into a text of woman/writing."[26]

Before concluding this article on two Japanese woman writers who may have been made scapegoats by the Japanese gender system, let us strike a positive note.

The fake angel, the figure with plastic wings, may transform into the "twittering machine" of paradise, as in a watercolor by Yagawa's favorite artist Paul Klee, who left a series of angel figures, most of which were created in his last years. The two Japanese daughters of Anaïs Nin will join their symbolic mother in a celestial chorus, just as Yagawa depicted a chorus of female voices in *Rabbit* ("Three women make a chorus!"), and sing/speak the "language of our mothers' land."[27]

In fact, they never stop speaking in this world as well, as long as we read their works (none of which is translated into English, unfortunately). The third and latest posthumous publication by Yagawa is a translation of Nin's *Little Birds*.[28] There is a project under way to publish Meio's collected essays on Anaïs Nin later this year, and hopefully there are many more voices to come. ◈

Notes

[1] Noriko Mizuta writes: "The news of Ms. Masako Meio's abrupt death came as a great shock to me. Somehow it resembled a feeling of regret, an urge to stop her as soon as possible, if it had not been too late." (Translation mine, as all the other translations from Japanese to English are in this article.) "Fuyu e mukatte no Tabidachi" ("A Departure for Winter") in Meio, *Yuki Mukae (Snow-Welcoming)*. Tokyo: Kawade Shobo Shinsha, 1995. 261-265.

[2] Hara, Masako. "Anaïs Nin no Musume-tachi" ("The Daughters of Anaïs Nin"), *Bokushin 9*, 1977. 8-21.

[3] Butler, Judith. *Bodies That Matter*. NY: Routledge, 1993. 153.

[4] Meio, Masako. *Aru Onna no Glimpse (A Glimpse of a Woman)*. Tokyo: Kodan-sha, 1999. 42.

[5] Ibid. 104.

[6] Ueno, Chizuko. *Onna to iu Kairaku (The Pleasure That Is Woman)*. Tokyo: Keisô Shobô, 1986. 16.

[7] http://web.princeton.edu/sites/sics/speakers.htm

[8] She studied a year in the US in 1957 as an exchange student for AFS, majored in English literature as an undergraduate and graduate student in Japan, and spent another year in the US when Kojin Karatani was a visiting scholar at Yale. This American/English experience had a great influence on the shaping of her sense of split/multiple identities.

[9] Yamashita, Etsuko. "Josei no Jiritsu to Haha-teki Jubaku no Genkai" ("Women's Independence and the Limit of Maternal Bind"). *Tokyo Shinbun*, 24 Apr. 1996, late ed.

[10] Nin, Anaïs. *The Diary of Anaïs Nin, Vol. 1*. Ed. Gunther Stuhlmann. San Diego: Harcourt, 1966. 204.

[11] Butler. *Gender Trouble: Feminism and the Subversion of Identity*. NY: Routledge, 1990. 33.

[12] Hara, Akie. "Yakusha Atogaki" ("Translator's Note"), *Anaïs Nin no Nikki* (1931-34). Tokyo: Chikuma-shobo, 1991. 643.

[13] Millet, Kate. "Anaïs—A Mother to Us All," *ANAIS: An International Journal* vol. 9, 1991.

[14] Nin. *Children of the Albatross, Cities of the Interior*. Chicago: Swallow Press, 1974. 160.

[15] The wife of a famous Japanese sculptor/poet Kôtarô Takamura. She had an artistic talent and was one of the "new women" in modern Japan, but later suffered from a nervous breakdown. Kôtarô's most popular book of poems, *Chieko-shô*, is written about his mentally ill wife.

[16] Nin. *The Diary of Anaïs Nin, Vol. 2*. Ed. Gunther Stuhlmann. New York: Harcourt/Swallow, 1967. 233.

[17] Yagawa, Sumiko. *Alice in the Wordland,* in *Yagawa Sumiko Sakuhisn Shûsei (The Collected Works of Sumiko Yagawa).* Tokyo: Shoshi Yamada, 1999. 133-192.

[18] Mizuta, Noriko. "Shôjo to iu Bunshin" ("The Girl as a Double"). Ed. Eiji Sikine, in *Uta no Hibikiki Monogatari no Yokubo.* Tokyo: Shinwa-sha, 1996. 132.

[19] Yagawa. *Anaïs Nin no Shôjo Jidai (Anaïs Nin as a Young Girl).* Tokyo: Kawade Shobô Shinsha, 2002. 19.

[20] Yagawa. *Usagi to Yobareta Onna (A Woman Called Rabbit)* in *Sakuhin Shûsei.* 267.

[21] Ibid. 265.

[22] Yagawa. "Itsumo Sobani Honga" ("Books Always by My Side"), *Asahi Shinbun,* Feb. 10, 2002.

[23] Yagawa. *Ushinawareta Niwa (The Lost Garden)* in *Sakuhin Shûsei.* 568, 570.

[24] *Bookish* 2 (2002): 49-55.

[25] *Asahi Shinbun,* Feb. 17, 2002.

[26] Spivak, Gayatri Chakravorty. *A Critique of Postcolonial Reason.* Cambridge: Harvard UP. 308.

[27] Yagawa. *Usagi* in *Sakuhin Shusei.* 277.

[28] Nin. *Kotori-tachi.* Trans. Yagawa. Tokyo: Shinchô-sha, 2003.

The women of Japan are at once the most present and the most invisible and elusive inhabitants of any country I have seen. They were everywhere, in restaurants, streets, shops, museums, subways, trains, fields, hotels and inns, and yet achieved a self-effacement which, to foreign women, is striking. In the hotels and inns they were solicitous, thoughtful. It was as if one's dream of an ever-attentive, ever-protective mother were fulfilled on a collective scale, only the mother is forever young and daintily dressed. They were laborious and yet quiet, efficient, ever present and yet not intrusive or cumbersome.

What kind of modern woman would emerge from the deep, masked, long-hidden Japanese woman of old? The whole mystery of Japanese women lay behind their smooth faces, which rarely showed age except perhaps on peasant women battered by nature. The smoothness remained from childhood far into maturity.

There is a strong tendency to live according to the code, the mores, the religious or cultural rules, to live for a collective ideal. The one who breaks away is described as a monster of evil (Diary 7, 6-8).

Philip K. Jason

Adventures in the Nin Trade
A look back at a career in Nin scholarship

S ome ten or so years ago, at about the same time that I was preparing *Anaïs Nin and Her Critics* for Camden House, I proposed a book that would collect my own essays on Nin and weave a career narrative—the story of my own "Nin Career"— around and through them. The book would thus be the illustrated story of one scholar's engagement with an author's work over a period of three decades. Now it's a story of over four decades, which I will present here in abbreviated form. It is a story told by a just-retired college professor who met Nin's work as an undergraduate student and, more or less, fell in love.

It is also a story that began again recently when I received a call from a total stranger—a man named Steven Fazio—who had discovered that I resided in Naples, Florida and wanted to sit down with me to have some serious conversation about Nin on one of his regular trips to my town from his home in Tampa. He had discovered Nin through my *Anaïs Nin Reader* (1973), and he had collected and read and studied her writings ever since. He had found a link to my home page on an Anaïs Nin web page. The Internet provides the latest version of the widening circle impulse, set in motion so many years ago by the Richard Centing and Ben Franklin V newsletter *Under the Sign of Pisces: Anaïs Nin and Her Circle.* This periodical was the first respectable home for the discussion of Nin's work, and it launched the careers of most Nin scholars of that generation, including myself. I hope to sit down with Steven soon.

But my story, like Steven Fazio's, begins with the excited discovery of Nin's writing, a discovery that quickly led to infatuation.

It began during the academic year 1960-1961 when I came upon the then-new Swallow Press editions of Nin's work in Greenwich Village bookshops. At nineteen, I was smitten. In a letter dated some ten years later (May 28, 1971), writing to her from Georgetown University, I told a version of the tale to Nin herself:

Dear Miss Nin,
    Let me begin by telling you a little story: a variation on a theme you've no doubt heard many times before.
    After some false starts at the University of Maryland, finally finding my proper vocation to be literary study, I uprooted myself

and in the fall of 1960 moved to New York to attend the New School for Social Research. At that school and around Greenwich Village many new vistas opened before me. I began to feel that the psychological approach to literary art was most congenial for me (through courses taught by such men as Gerald Sykes); I began to explore my own potential as a writer; and, in the 8th Street bookshops, discovered the Swallow editions of your works. Intrigued, I avidly read your books as they became available to me, studied them, began to compile notes, and followed your career through the succeeding ten years.

I didn't tell Nin then of the amazing piece of luck that came my way at a used bookstore near the 92nd Street YM/WHA where I found, for 25 cents, a copy of the Gemor Press *Under a Glass Bell* (1944) that is still in my collection. Was it fate?

The letter continues:

Along the way, I obtained my B.A., M.A., and now my Ph.D. This formal study kept my continuing interest from reaching any useful issue, but I knew all that while that part of my career—an important part—would be dedicated to teaching and writing about your work. The first real opportunity came this past fall when I was able to include *A Spy in the House of Love* in one of my courses. From this came an essay soon to appear [in truncated form] in the newsletter that Mr. Centing has been editing.

From here, the letter pitches the idea of the *Anaïs Nin Reader*, the story of which I have already told in my memoir of Nin that appears in Benjamin Franklin V's *Recollections of Anaïs Nin by Her Contemporaries* (1996).

Those ten years between the discovery of Nin's work and the initiation of a career as a Nin scholar were frustrating years in which I found few people with whom to share my enthusiasm for her writing. I did, indeed, compile an impressive, if informal, bibliography of primary and secondary sources that served me well later on. I read otherwise unavailable titles in the Rare Book Room at the Library of Congress. In fact, sometime during that decade, I went to hear Nin give a talk at the LC. All the while, her poetic prose moved me. It fed the romantic side of my sensibilities during a very late adolescence and through early adulthood. It countered my graduate school studies in 18th Century British Literature—"The Age of Reason." When Nin's Djuna struck up vaguely erotic and potentially liberating relationships with young men too mired in reason (or at least "authority") for their own good, I vicariously joined the entourage. I admired and required the lesson of personal evolution, of change and growth, of stability's dangers, of the need for a youthful perspective that defies limitation. I still do.

When the time came, in the early 1970s, to declare myself a Nin scholar, there was little in this identity to commend me to the academic world. Pieces in *Pisces*, a review essay on Evelyn Hinz's trailblazing book[*] in *The Journal of the Otto Rank Association*, a review of *Diary 4* in the *Washington Post*—these small efforts led to the *Reader* and, over time, to a series of Nin projects through which I found myself peculiarly positioned. Meanwhile, the work of other scholars helped build Nin study into a respectable field, though even today a marginal one.

While I always admired her work—and parts, at least, of her exemplary life in art—I more and more found her writing uneven and limited. I wanted to join with others in praising her worth, but I did not find it possible to be uncritical. I could not deify her. After a while, I found myself a reluctant partisan, locked in battles with people I labeled (privately?) as sycophants. I remember speaking out after a series of enthusiastic papers at a Modern Language Association meeting (in New York, I believe), and getting verbally pelted by the majority on hand. To raise questions or doubts about the stature of Nin's achievement or the rigor of argument behind another scholar's fulsome praise was to be in the wrong room. But I felt that to over-praise was, in the long run, to do Nin's art a disservice.

These issues came up in my own reviewing, both of Sharon Spencer's book[†] and Nancy Scholar's.[‡] At least with Scholar I had found a "bad guy" whose Nin-bashing far exceeded my own. Next to hers, my reservations seemed (and are) quite tame.

No career, or even career strand, is without disappointments. Though I feel fortunate to have earned a place of some prominence in the ongoing conversation about Nin's life and art, I've met with several setbacks. There is no need to present a whiny catalogue—I'll only mention here my failure to complete a project into which I invested considerable time at the UCLA library and elsewhere. I had noticed, imbedded in Nin's manuscript diaries, a series of letters from Rank to Nin, only a small portion of which had been published. Though I transcribed them and was prepared to publish them with an introduction, I was never able to obtain the necessary permission.

---

[*] The Mirror and the Garden, *Ohio State University Libraries (1971).—Ed.*

[†] Collage of Dreams, *Swallow Press (1977).—Ed.*

[‡] Anaïs Nin, *Gale Group (1984).—Ed.*

Because that relationship had already become a primary concern of my scholarship, I felt an intense frustration. Looking back, this feeling has diminished to a minor irritation.

In my central writings, I found it useful to pursue my original attraction: the psychological dimensions of Nin's art. I wrote less—through the seventies and eighties—about her shortcomings as a writer and more about what she drew upon, how her fictions worked, what key personality dynamics they probed, and the genre issues regarding the border between fiction and autobiography. My contributions to the special 1978 issue of *Mosaic* ("Doubles/Don Juans: Anaïs Nin and Otto Rank") and to Sharon Spencer's 1986 anthology* ("The Princess and the Frog: Anaïs Nin and Otto Rank") kept me out of arguments about the measure of Nin's esthetic achievement. But it wasn't long before I was gauging my position in the next battle: Nin's stature as a truth-teller. My comments on the *Henry and June* volume ("Dropping Another Veil" in *ANAIS: An International Journal,* vol. 6, 1988) engaged this issue.

Along the way, I realized that these critical arguments had a much longer history than I had suspected. I discovered that the shape of Nin's career—her critical reception and its meaning—was a fascinating story in itself.

One job that had to be done was to pin down certain aspects of that career: those that had to do with networking and self-publishing. This interest in the sociology and economics of literary production actually had its roots in my long-abandoned interest in Restoration and 18th Century British Theatre. Here, I had done work on the situation of the playwright: how plays were selected, how theatrical bills were determined, how playwrights were paid, and related matters. Art has a social and economic context that is often disregarded. In the case of Nin, I prepared a careful study on "The Gemor Press" that appeared in *ANAIS: An International Journal*, vol. 2 (1984). I followed it up one year later with a "networking" story: "Oscar Baradinsky's 'Outcasts: Henry Miller, Anaïs Nin, Maya Deren and the Alicat Bookshop Press.'" Later came "A Delicate Battle Cry: Nin's Pamphlets of the 1940s" (*ANAIS: An International Journal*, vol. 8, 1990), which is of bibliographical interest and provides a glance at Nin's early esthetic self-positioning. She was, in these works and elsewhere, attempting to establish the grounds for the critical debate that would swirl around her. To my dismay, many critics would appeal to Nin's self-justifications rather than bring other relevant criteria of judgment to bear on the assessment of her work.

---

*Anaïs, Art and Artists: a Collection of Essays, *Penkevill (1987).—Ed.*

It had become clear by now that one of my major areas of contribution to Nin studies would be to examine the debate itself. The 1993 issue of *ANAIS: An International Journal* included my "Issues in Nin Criticism," a preliminary borrowing from the monograph *Anaïs Nin and Her Critics* that appeared the same year. My goal there had been to read everything and act as a fair referee. Nonetheless, I didn't work too hard, or hard enough, at hiding my prejudices. Having prepared myself to perform the task of tracing Nin's career by mapping out the history of critical responses, I was more than ready to produce a companion effort. The collection of essays titled *The Critical Response to Anaïs Nin* (1996) essentially completed that project. A retrospective gathering, the book is designed to represent the range of positions on Nin's work over six decades. For me it was the matching bookend to the selection of Nin's own work published twenty-three years earlier.

For all of this interest in stepping back to define the Nin story in these ways, I haven't fully resisted the temptation to return to her works and to comment on them. Two companion pieces of 1997 explore what Nin reveals and hides, where she succeeds and where she (pardon me once again) fails. These are "The Burden of Self: Some Thoughts on *The Early Diary of Anaïs Nin, 1927-1931*" (*ANAIS: An International Journal*, vol. 15, 1997) and "The Men in Nin's (Characters') Lives," which is included in Suzanne Nalbantian's *Anaïs Nin: Literary Perspectives* (1997). Also, in my ongoing fool's errand to have the last word about my topics, I have contributed many entries on Nin to major reference works and written review essays on the full-length biographies by Noel Riley Fitch and Deirdre Bair.

Yes, it is a fool's errand and a vain wish: to have the last word. It can't be done, yet I believe that most of us who work in the Nin trade and in other areas of literary study almost believe it can. In our wiser moments, we know that we are only players and that we contribute to a continuing process. If we didn't know this truth, even a superficial reading of Nin would set us straight—the art of "becoming." That's all we have, and it is everything: the possibility and power of transformation. The primary creative act of self-making, we learn, is an act that is all process and has no end before our death—and perhaps no end after our death, either. ◈

Benjamin Franklin V

Passing the Torch
The need for bibliographical updating of Anaïs Nin's work

he writing itself first attracted me to Anaïs Nin. I had just read *House of Incest* when the initial volume of the *Diary* was published in 1966. These works so appealed to me that I wanted to read everything she had written, which, in time, I did, thanks largely to Alan Swallow, who had recently published her books that had originally appeared in the 1930s, 1940s, and 1950s. The more I read, the more captivated I became, not only by the literature but also by the *Diary* persona named Anaïs Nin. It was the person/persona of Nin that initiated my life-long scholarly interest in her. In trying to locate information, I was stymied; almost nothing existed about her, other than brief mention in an occasional reference book, and the sources sometimes offered conflicting "facts." When was she born? Was she married? What, precisely, had she written? There were no easy answers.

After attempting to satisfy my curiosity, I began focusing on the question of what she had written. This was important because Duane Schneider and I had agreed to write a book about Nin's publications, and I wanted to know what they were before evaluating them. In *Under the Sign of Pisces: Anaïs Nin and Her Circle*, a newsletter Richard Centing and I edited, I wrote mostly about bibliographical issues. This interest resulted in the 1973 publication of my *Anaïs Nin: A Bibliography* with the Kent State University Press, a work she said she admired. What Anaïs wrote is also the focus of my essay in Robert Zaller's *A Casebook on Anaïs Nin* (1974). My bibliographical impulse remained, and remains, strong. Along the way, I have been able to detail the publications of the obscure Anaïs Nin Press, debunk the notion that she wrote *White Stains*—which has been attributed to her by more than one publisher—and address other issues about her publications that I hope benefit scholars and possibly readers who are not Nin specialists.

The most obvious bibliographical need is an updating of my three-decades-old bibliography, something someone else must do because of where I stand in my career: I have retired. ◈

thinking homes

T rying to touch you
with you gone so far away
i have turned the soil in your
strawberry patch, watered
the houseplants & monitored
filtered light on the african violet
washed all your cardigans
in the kitchen sink
and not pulled out a
single strand of long hair
tangled into each one of them
i have trellised your clematis
broomed the garage floor
smelt each new clustre on your
lilac bush; every night i've
built fresh sandwiches for
our moody teenager's school lunch
and in the long evenings
thinned out the tiny apples
and pinched off deadheads
from beds of irises and tulips
watching the thick leaves
on the sigvaldasons' manitoba maples
glisten in the fiery light of
reluctant prairie sunsets

the fuzzy chinese poppies
are readying to let loose
their crinkly orange blooms
already pink is bursting
through tight peony buds

> *i have to stop fooling*
> *myself—come back*
> *i want to touch your face*

> PS: I do hope the mimosas by the rickshaw tracks
> and the crimson-canopied *shimul* are comforting you
> a whole lot better; you were so keen to go 'home'. ◈

Dudley Levenson

Appreciating Gunther Stuhlmann
A man of letters—1927 - 2002

Gunther Stuhlmann passed away April 1, 2002, at his home in Becket, Massachusetts with his wife, Barbara, at his side. He designed and built his home, where he grew and nurtured a garden in the same careful manner that he cultivated a community of artists and writers in the Berkshires and abroad.

At 6'6" with a white moustache, mirthful eyes, and a questioning German intellect, he was a prominent observer of culture and a distinguished voice among artful minds in New York, the Berkshires, and internationally. Although he devoted long hours to research and reading manuscripts in the book-lined sanctuary of his home office, he delighted in visiting local art galleries, museums, and dance performances. He was involved with local cultural organizations, as well as representing various authors and publishing a literary journal, *ANAIS: An International Journal*.

Gunther's observations in the *International Journal* were the work of an insightful reader who had studied the life and times of Anaïs Nin and her sphere. He not only knew her personally, he was her literary agent for years. He explored the uncharted territory of her inner life by reading the journals before they were published, and then helped introduce all of us to her work. His selection of material and informative notes in the *International Journal* helped clarify many of Anaïs's more complex issues and connect readers to related writings.

Those who have read Gunther Stuhlmann's column, "Appreciating African Art" for the magazine *The Artful Mind* will miss his intelligent investigation into the origins and meanings of art from another continent. He would choose a theme, then hunt down the best writings and latest publications on the subject. The articles were part book review and part personal observation, often after viewing a museum collection. He recommended volumes that were "rich in investigative and interpretive detail." His mission was to assist the reader in gaining a broader perspective on a creative genre that contrasts with contemporary aesthetics but resonates with human experience.

Gunther had more than a scholar's appreciation for African art, he had a passionate interest. He had an excellent collection of African sculpture, masks, ornaments, and ritual objects in his home. When he learned about the identity or meaning of a piece, he wanted to share the knowledge. Each time I visited the Stuhlmann house, many of the

African figures were arranged differently. Some were brought to the entryway to greet people at the door, while others were gathered around the dining room table to amuse and give honor to the meal—a spicy bean stew with a salad of white asparagus. Many of the figures were facing each other as if talking, taking part in a ritual or a romantic encounter. Often the statues were laden with exotic beads leading me to think that Barbara had a hand in these artistic interactions.

After dinner we always talked about books. The latest books on African art would be laid out on the couch or Gunther would select a volume from the shelf and open it to illustrate an African theme he was exploring. The discussions glided freely to the influence of African art on modern painting and sculpture, the Picasso exhibit in New York, then segued to the French surrealists, a Dostoyevsky novel, a relevant article in the current *New York Times Review of Books*. Barbara and Gunther shared anecdotes about the crowd of artists and writers they knew in New York, California, and Europe.

Gunther grew up in prewar Germany and was a teenager during the war. When I asked what he did during the war, he shook his head, "Those were confused and fearful times. I was not political, I had to try to survive." His family and his friends, many of whom were Jews and independent minded intellectuals, never imagined the Nazis ("a fringe group of blockheads") would come to such devastating power. Although Gunther started medical school, he became interested in the theatre. After working for a liberal publishing firm in Berlin, (*Encounter* magazine, *The Works of Thomas Mann*, etc.), he followed his dream to New York in 1950. He lived in Greenwich Village on a shoestring, spending time with artists and writers in Provincetown, participating in the Bohemian community of painters, actors, and poets who shared meals, materials, and ideas. He started a literary agency. Tom Berger was one of his original clients and an early triumph with *Little Big Man*, which was also made into a movie. Berger recalls that when his first book, *Crazy in Berlin* came out, Gunther gave him the best party, waltzing through the crowd with a parakeet on his shoulder, pouring screwdrivers. Imagine another scene from the 50s—Gunther whooping it up with Jack Kerouac and other beat characters in the back of a smoked-filled jalopy.

B.H. Friedman remembers Gunther "on the scene in New York." He was "very intelligent in his reading of my manuscripts." Gunther represented Friedman's prose poem, "Whispers," originally published in Saul Bellow's *Noble Savage* as a response to Allen Ginsberg's "Howl." Friedman wrote a deep analysis of abstract expressionist Jackson Pollack, who studied with the conservative American painter, Thomas Hart Benton. (Pollack eventually rebelled against Benton's reactionary politics and style of art.) *Energy Made Visible* was well received and Gunther promoted it for a film.

"Even when Gunther didn't make any money, he stuck with me. He was not a very commercial person. That was what I liked about him. He was more literary, more sympathetic; I felt very loyal to him," says Friedman.

Gunther met Anaïs Nin in 1954. Nin, after returning to New York City from Paris at the onset of World War II, had been printing her own books because of New York publishers' indifference to her writing. In Gunther she found a strong supporter. At the time he became her agent, Anaïs and her husband, filmmaker and engraver Ian Hugo, were living in the Village off Washington Square. Having been an influential muse to Henry Miller in Paris, he gave her the rights to publish his letters to her. Gunther was the editor of that correspondence, and *Letters to Anaïs Nin* came out in 1965. *A Literate Passion*, which included her letters to Miller, came out in 1987. Her *Diaries*, which she began at age eleven as letters of longing to her absent father, became what some consider to be an imaginative documentation of a life in art and a personal transformation, in which she found her literary voice. When Anaïs and Gunther decided to publish the *Diaries*, he suggested that her story commence in 1931, the year she published her first book in France, a study of D.H. Lawrence, and stepped forward as a writer. *The Diary of Anaïs Nin* came out in 1966 during the upward swing of the Women's Liberation Movement. Six more volumes followed, all edited by Gunther.

In 1983 critically acclaimed novelist, Richard Powers, sent Gunther an inquiry on his manuscript *Three Farmers on Their Way to a Dance*. Gunther replied with enthusiasm and said with wry humor that he thought he might find a buyer for the book. When Richard asked about making a contract first, Gunther replied, "Life's too short for a contract. We'll find out soon enough if we get along." Get along they did, for almost twenty years of books.

Powers says, "He was with me since the beginning. He put the human touch before business formality. He was straightforward and you always knew where you stood with him." Powers recalls their relationship, "He trusted me. He was a fatherly figure, the father that looks out for you, who gives you advance warning and steps aside so you do what you have to do. He was a model of honesty and integrity, what I needed between me and New York. I needed someone who believed in me. He would say helpful things about the kind of audience and how they would receive the book, and he was always right."

Gunther and Barbara Stuhlmann
Photo © Sky Blue Press

Richard Powers went on to write *The Gold Bug Variations, Operation Wandering Soul, Galatea 2.2,* and *Plowing the Dark.*

In the sixties, Gunther met Barbara, who was working in New York City for the *Times of London.* He told Tom Berger that he had met "a brilliant and talented young woman who is as beautiful as Julie Christie." They married in 1966 and lived in an apartment with a roof garden on Irving Place and 18th Street near his offices. For seven years each spring he took her to Europe, where they would meet authors and publishers in London, Munich, Hamburg, Barcelona, the French Riviera, and then retire to drink wine at Parisian Cafés.

After years of dealings and parties in New York, Gunther and Barbara began to think about getting a place in the country. They signed up for driving lessons so they could explore New England. Robin Carson, a Greenwich Village character who had photographed Billie Holiday in the 30s, told Gunther about the Berkshires where he had a "shack." He claimed that the country wasn't so remote— "Pittsfield has fourteen first run movie theaters." The shack turned out to be a charming two-story farmhouse, which Gunther and Barbara visited in 1975. Three hours seemed like a good distance from the city, so they hunted and found land just down the road on a wooded hillside, where they set up a tent on the knoll. Gunther learned to cook over a wood fire, and they would share a jug of wine, listening to Tanglewood on the radio. He planted a vegetable garden before the construction began on the house. Barbara remembers him designing the house at his desk in New York—"a simple and efficient place just for us." They built the house in 1976. "Our health improved up here with all the activity, using our muscles, the clean air. Gunther got in shape using the chain saw. Coming out of the city, people only knew him as a bar-hopper and a party-goer. They couldn't imagine him as a country guy. But the gardens and the daffodils were his creations."

Making a home and a garden were wholesome projects, but they soon got involved with the community as well. Gunther served with the

Cultural Council, which is a state agency that awards art grants, and the Becket Arts Center, a hilltown agency that sponsors exhibits, lectures and music programs. He wrote for *The Artful Mind* during the last four years before his death. Gunther and Barbara often had lunch at local cafés, where conversation ran from this year's sugar snap crop to the latest performance at Jacob's Pillow.

Gunther continued his job as a literary agent. According to Richard Powers, "He was devoted to his authors. He liked to talk about my books after they were published; he made connections that I hadn't thought of." Gunther coordinated an international community of Anaïs Nin readers, scholars, psychoanalysts, and artists—people touched by the life and work of Nin—by editing *ANAIS: An International Journal* from 1983 to 2001, when he became ill.

The acute leukemia advanced rapidly. Upon hearing his illness was terminal, Gunther said, "This is like wartime." Barbara was with him; they encouraged each other. I visited Gunther on his deathbed. The giant lay very still, then slowly opened his eyes and spoke something very softly about being on a threshold. He had always been so articulate, but now I could see the exhaustion from pain, the coming of peaceful silence after a life fully lived. He apologized for being too weak to talk. I told him he had already said so much, given so much.

The morning Gunther died, the mailbox he and Barbara had since the beginning of their new lives in the country, collapsed. The old wooden post was ready to go and it keeled over. A neighbor helped Barbara set it up again. Later, when Barbara went into the cellar, she found books that Gunther had stashed, including *The Tibetan Book of Living and Dying*. In our many conversations about classical and indigenous cultures, Gunther and I touched upon spirituality, what he called the "unfamiliar but fascinating spiritual universe and its visible manifestations," but we hadn't focused on personal belief systems. We acknowledged the converging rivers of art and meaning in a world of entangled realities. It was something to appreciate in cerebral and simple ways—thinking philosophically while living in the countryside. Gunther remembered when, as a child, his kindhearted Uncle Julius would take him into the woods to commune with Nature.

Gunther Stuhlmann was a man of letters who read with great understanding and wrote clearly about deep artistic perceptions. He pored over texts, extracting the kernel of truth, the relevance of a passage. He loved hunting for African art and then devoted himself to illuminating the "intimate relationships between created object and the underlying beliefs, which determined their form and efficacy." He sparked his writers without inhibiting their own voices. He grew and nurtured his garden and his community. ◈

Travels and excursions

Paul Herron

Revisiting Anaïs Nin's France
Neuilly-sur-Seine and Louveciennes

Anaïs Nin's birthplace 100 years later

"Anaïs Nin was born February 21, 1903 in Neuilly, France." I have lost track of how many times I have read this passage without giving it much thought. Paris, Louveciennes, New York, and Los Angeles have always been at the top of any list of primary Nin locations, subject to scrutiny and research, but never have I seen much about Neuilly-sur-Seine, which some described at the turn of the 20th Century as "Paris's most fashionable suburb." On a recent visit to France, I decided to see if there remained anything palpable that could be affixed to what has become a mere footnote in Nin lore.

The first task was to find out exactly where the Nin house stood (if indeed it still did), and having done a bit of research, I found the address: 7 rue du Général-Henrion-Bertier. On the Internet, I discovered that this same address is home to an online shoestore, so there was a possibility that on the site I would find a steel and glass shop instead of a house worthy of Anaïs Nin's birth.

The short ride from Paris began by taking the No. 1 Métro line, direction La Défense, to the Pont-Neuilly stop. As I exited into the brilliant but cold February sunlight, I was greeted by a dazzling square on avenue Charles De Gaulle. Looking east, I could see the Arc de Triomphe in the distance; looking west, there was a different sort of "arc," that of La Défense, surrounded by its futuristic towers—in one direction, the past, and in the other, the future. In the middle of the square sits a fountain with a sculpture of the mythical character Sisyphus endlessly pushing a boulder uphill. Although the fountain was silent with winter, the expression on the face of the figure in its center echoed the famous reinterpretation of the myth by Camus.[1]

I followed my hand-written notes: walk west on Charles De Gaulle, turn left onto rue de Madrid, then right on rue du Général-Henrion-Bertier.[2] Along the way, I noted shops and restaurants filled with well-dressed businessmen and women, and the people on the street, young and old alike, exemplified the word "*chic*." When I turned onto rue du Général-Henrion-Bertier, the buildings seemed pre-1900, an appropriate age for Anaïs Nin to have been born in one of them, and they were well-kept. The street was somewhat commercial near rue de Madrid, with a bistro on the corner and a few shops farther down, but as I continued walking it metamorphosed into an established residential neighborhood, decorated with very expensive automobiles, the size of which are not to be found on the curbs of Paris.

After a few minutes, I looked back in the direction from which I'd come...it was the sort of path one takes when lost in dreams: the outside disappears, and one enters what seems to be a world of its own—this street seemed like a secret. The noise of the traffic had faded, the bustle yielding to a timeless, reflective silence.

Neuilly-sur-Seine took its name only six years before Nin's birth but has a history that dates back to the 13th Century when it was a small port along the Seine, 8 km west of Paris-Notre-Dame. Its days of grandeur included the construction of the Château de Madrid in the 16th Century, reflecting the power and extravagance of French royalty. Its days of turbulence saw the same Château demolished by revolutionaries in 1795, and Hitler's occupation of the city in the 1940s. Throughout much of its recent history, Neuilly has prided itself with its well-to-do inhabitants, its beautiful architecture, its surroundings (the Bois de Boulogne, the Seine, La Défense), and its superior quality of life.[3] It was the aristocratic setting for some of Colette's novels, *Cheri* in particular.

Joaquín Nin y Castellanos, Anaïs's father, by nature a disproportionately extravagant man, wished to live in Neuilly after leaving Cuba with his new wife, Rosa. Rosa argued it was more financially prudent to rent an apartment in St-Germain-des-Prés, where they lived briefly. Shortly before Anaïs was born, they made the move to Neuilly. The young family spent little time there, however, since much of Anaïs's first year or two was lived in hotels while her parents did musical tours together across Europe. A few years later, they moved to St-Cloud (another well-to-do suburb), reducing Neuilly to a childhood memory for Anaïs.

In *Diary 1*, she attempts to explain her obsession with walking along railway tracks:

> *Does this fascination for a possible accident come from the traumatic time when I missed such a death as a child? We had a servant in Neuilly (when I was two years old, and my brother Thorvald just born). My father must have seduced her and then forgotten her. Anyway, she sought revenge. She took my brother*

*and me on an outing and left the carriage, and me beside it, in the
middle of the railroad track. But the signal gateman saw us, and as
he had seven children of his own, he took a chance on his own life
and rushed out in time to kick the carriage out of the way and
carry me off in his arms. The event remained in our memory. I still
remember the beds covered with toys for the seven children of the
man who saved our lives (5-6).*

It is interesting to note that in the unpublished diary of the early
1940s, it is perhaps this same story that gets a twist from Anaïs's
mother:

*She told me an anecdote about my father when he was a very
young man. He made love to the maid in his house. She got
pregnant. He had to reveal this to his mother so as to get the
money for the abortion. The abortion was made. My father was
given the two month fetus in a shoe box to throw away into the sea.
He did not throw it away. He got dressed in black, with a black tie,
mourning costume, and took the box to all the cafés to show his
friends. "See, it's my child. I killed it. And I'm mourning for him."*

In *Diary 1*, she tells her analyst René Allendy:

*I have lost everyone I ever cared for. Every house, every country I
loved. First I loved our house in Neuilly. I was very sociable then. I
was four years old and I would go out in the street and invite
everybody for tea (115).*

In *Diary 2*, with World War II looming, Nin recounts her eerie
revisit to Neuilly with her houseboat, *La Belle Aurore*:

*One morning I found in my letter box an order from the river
police to move out of Paris. All the houseboats had been asked to
move out. I had to rent a tugboat to pull my houseboat further up
the Seine... We were out of Paris. We passed under a bridge and
reached a factory section. We passed another bridge and reached
a boatyard, filled with skeletons of old barges, rusty anchors. A
cemetery for boats. They advised me as I passed to continue up to
Neuilly. There was room to anchor there. Neuilly! I had
circumnavigated only to return to my birthplace. An omen? And
my father, too, moved to Neuilly, near where he had lived when I
was born (303).*

Her father was then living in a "comfortable modern place for retired persons" overlooking a cemetery, "which to a Spaniard is a fatal omen." She mentions also that during a walk in the Bois:

> [H]e was gently reminiscing about the days when he took my brother and me to play in the same park... [He said,] "In this very park I took you walking when you were a child. I could have been happy as a father, a husband, a musician, if I had not been obsessed with winning more and more women" (304).

Ironically, it was from Neuilly that Joaquín Nin would return to Cuba, where he lived out his last years in poverty.

I continued my search on the narrow, deserted street—not a car, not a pedestrian walking a dog. The low winter sun brightly illuminated the buildings on the street, bathing them in warmth and stunning brightness. It didn't take long to reach number 7, which was on the

7 rue du Général-Henrion-Bertier.
Photo © Sky Blue Press

south side of the street. No, it was not a shoestore. It was instead an elegant five-story building, warm and rich in its appearance, like a miniature version of the châteaux destroyed during the revolution. Several families could (and most likely do) live within its confines. The bottom portion of each side window is decorated with an ornate cast iron grate. The windows on the two front corners are balconied semi-circles tracing their turret-like towers. The front windows also sport balconies, as do most of the penthouse windows. The house is built out of stone, as most buildings in Paris are, and it possesses distinction despite the fact there is a sister building next door. It is easy to see why someone as socially conscious as Joaquín Nin would be attracted to this place, and why Anaïs remembered it the way she did. I could almost imagine the Proustian figures emerging from behind their heavy leaded glass doors to peer down at the precocious little girl who had just invited them to tea. In fact, one has to wonder whether the essence of Anaïs Nin's memories of this neighborhood had something to do with her fascination with Proust.

On this particular winter day, however, paper snowflakes taped to the inside of one of the windows were evidence of children living at 7 rue du Général-Henrion-Bertier. Perhaps they will never be aware of the little daughter of Cuban artists who once lived there, but then again, one can be certain they are filling the rooms with their own music, with their own dreams, creating their own memories.

Louveciennes: New life at 2 bis rue de Montbuisson

I will never forget the first time I visited Louveciennes. I was in search of Anaïs Nin's legendary house, but I was ill-prepared, having no address, no helpful information. It was a gray February day in 1992, and once I got off the train, I realized I had no idea where to go next, no clue where the house was, figuring that I would "somehow" find it, leaving the rest to fate. The deserted streets looked foreboding, so I simply started walking toward the *centre-ville*, hoping I wasn't embarking on an impossible quest. I encountered a couple taking a stroll and asked for directions. To my surprise, neither of them had ever heard of Anaïs, let alone knew where the house was (I later discovered that practically no one in Louveciennes knows who Anaïs Nin is). They took me to the town historian and art expert, Jacques Laÿ, who, with his wife Monique, had recently published *Louveciennes Mon Village*, a comprehensive book of Louvecienne's history and personages. Jacques, after making good fun of my French, directed us to the house, which was in a state of horrible disrepair and was often invaded by kids doing drugs or vagrants. It was at a crossroads then: to demolish it, or to restore it. The asking price was formidable: $1.5 million, enough to keep most buyers away, especially since at least that much would be needed to repair it. The windows were broken, the trellis was falling from the walls, the courtyard was unkempt and ugly. It had an aura, though, a sort of intangible allure, as though it had been empty since the day Anaïs left but her life there had been absorbed by the walls. I was at once awed and haunted. For weeks afterward, I would dream of the empty house, of the sun traversing its path across the rotting floors every day, of faint echoes from the past, of the walls shaking from electrical storms and the broken windows allowing the rain to flood the rooms. I dreamt of an empty slab of stone behind the gate, the house gone forever.

I returned to Louveciennes twice during the next two years to visit my new friends, always making time to see the Nin house. I was aware of being watched by a hostile-looking old woman, who peered out of one of the windows of the dungeon-like house next door. Once, she appeared at one of the nearly bricked up windows and hollered "*Je vais appeler la police!*" when I was sticking my camera through the bars of the gate. It turns out this sinister individual was the reclusive and terribly obstinate owner of the Nin house, someone without the resources to make it livable, and yet vehemently opposed to any plan that involved a second party. In fact, this was same woman who turned Anaïs herself away the last time she visited Louveciennes.[4]

In 1994, I managed to "break into" the courtyard with the help of Jacques and Pierre Lescure, the novelist who lived down the street. I'll never forget the experience. M. Lescure, who was not well, suddenly decided during a visit at his house that we must go look at the Nin house and find out just exactly what was going on there. "We're going to get to the bottom of this," he said in impeccable British English, referring to why no one seemed to be fixing the place up. He was dressed in pajamas and a nightcap, his gray hair sticking wildly out from underneath. Despite discouragement from his wife and us, he pulled on a pair of green rubber knee-boots, threw on a robe, and stepped boldly out onto the street. It was mid-afternoon and very warm. The three of us strode down the middle of the street to the Nin house, as if we were in a surrealistic and tragic cowboy movie, M. Lescure leading the way with fire in his eyes. We drew stares from passersby. There was a temporary blue gate at the Nin house, a cheap rendition of the original, which totally blocked our view. M. Lescure went to the pedestrian gate and rang the bell! Of course, there was no answer and he was clearly peeved. Next, we walked to the big gate, and Jacques gave it a good shove. It was unlocked and groaned horribly as it opened. Luckily, the old lady was nowhere in sight. We went into the courtyard, walking almost in slow motion, looking about as if we'd just landed on an uncharted planet. Jacques exclaimed, "What a shame," when the decay of the house and grounds could be seen from close up. "What a terrible, terrible shame." We looked into one of the windows. The room looked exactly as it had in my dreams—empty and decrepit. Piles of trash here and there, broken pieces of wood and glass strewn about the filthy floor. We left, dejected. I didn't return for eight years.

I recall a well-intentioned scholar, Lori Wood, who had begun a drive to restore the house to its grandeur of the thirties and to turn it into a "home" and library/atalier for visiting artists, but she met the same resistance from the same owner and eventually abandoned the idea. Another crusader, another young American woman, got into the mix in the mid-nineties, trying to block the sale of the house (the old lady may have died by that time) and coordinate efforts to raise enough money to buy it and to turn it into something similar to Lori Wood's vision. These efforts ultimately failed, but fortunately the house was sold to a private individual who had enough money to fix it up again. While it is true the new owner split the property up for apartments to rent out and apparently had little interest in Anaïs Nin, the bottom line is that he saved the house from being destroyed. By the time I returned in 2002, the house was transformed. What remained of the trellis was completely torn down and the walls were repainted. The broken windows were replaced, the weeds were gone, and the original gate was restored and back in place—but it was still locked, and one still could not enter. Despite this, I was relieved the place was still standing, and moreover, there were people living in it once again.

In September 2002 Jacques wrote to me, excitedly telling me that the house had been sold again, this time to a French actor. Later, he found out more, telling me the actor was Jean-Hugues Anglade, star of "37°2 le Matin" and "La Reine Margot," and famous in France. Doing some research I found he'd been nominated for an Academy Award at one point and commands a large and devoted fan base. Louveciennes has always had a way of attracting leading artists and personalities: Madame du Barry (whose château still stands), Renoir, Alfred Sisley, Degas, Brigitte Bardot, and now Jean-Hugues Anglade.

A little later, Jacques, with the help of Anne-Marie Thomas, the Deputy Mayor of Louveciennes in charge of Culture, managed to secure a rendezvous with Jean-Hugues at his (Anaïs's) house. As a testament to Jacques' skill in such matters, he was able to schedule the visit for February 21, 2003, Anaïs's 100th birthday. After all the years of looking at the place from the outside, watching it slowly decay, fearing its demolition, and then seeing it come back from death, we would be able to enter, to walk around, explore, take pictures, not to mention enjoy the company of one of France's leading actors. As the date approached, I kept waiting for something awful to happen, like an airline strike, but amazingly nothing did.

Anne-Marie Thomas, we were told, had invited all the guests, including Geneviève Casile, who was one of Comédie-Française's most renowned members for decades, to her place to relax and chat before the visit to Jean-Hugues' house. My wife and I sent an invitation to Claudine Brelet, once a close friend of Lawrence Durrell, since through Durrell she naturally had acquired an interest in Anaïs. Claudine would provide a human link to the Villa Seurat trio, and the thought of having her at Anaïs's house for this occasion seemed almost mystical.

Once in Paris, after doing our usual book peddling at the bookstores, enjoying the cafés, and being guided through Montparnasse by Claudine, who is intimately knowledgeable about its neighborhoods and history, we prepared for Louveciennes. We met Claudine at the Métro station at Café Zeyer, a former Nin/Miller/Durrell hangout during the Villa Seurat days, and left for Gare St-Lazare. Gare St-Lazare looks exactly as it did when Renoir painted it in the 19th Century, except for the trains. It is the same station from which Anaïs, Henry, and a host of other *Diary* characters, left on their way to Louveciennes, the "laboratory of the soul," as Henry called it. The train ride takes a half-hour, just as it did seventy years ago. The stops are the same: St-Cloud, Bougival, Marly... The only blemish was graffiti, which has spread like an ugly weed, seemingly reaching farther and farther with each visit, this time all the way to Louveciennes.

We read *Diary* passages concerning Louveciennes aloud during the ride to mentally prepare ourselves for the big moment.

> *My house is two hundred years old. It has walls a yard thick, a big garden, a very large green iron gate for cars, flanked by a small green gate for people. The big garden is in the back of the house* (Diary 1, *3*).

I have always believed that part of the magic of France is that everything is a part of everything else. Art, music, literature, customs, language, food, drink, people, historical events and sites, are all interconnected, and never before had I felt it as strongly as during the train ride. Each "part" made the entire experience more powerful and meaningful. The *Diary* passages, the train itself, Paris, Café Zeyer, the flowers Claudine had purchased for the Laÿs, the glorious early afternoon sunshine, the growing anticipation—everything, all linked. We all felt it.

The train station in Louveciennes is the same as it has been for more than one hundred years (except now there is a restaurant next door that stylistically clashes with it, which Jacques calls "affreux"—frightful). Jacques met us in the parking lot, standing alone and proud, dressed to the nines, reminding us of the significance of our visit.

We lunched at the Laÿs', Monique having home-cooked a meal *"traditionnelement français,"* and we were blessed with more kinds of wine and cheese than I can possibly remember. The conversation was energetic as Jacques told stories particular to the area, myths, legends.

Jacques pointed to his watch and we were off to Anne-Marie's, a contemporary home on a hill, with a mechanically opening gate to which was affixed a sign that read "*chien lunatique*" (crazy dog). The *lunatique* turned out to be an old, huge Labrador Retriever, as slow and as gentle as a teddy bear. Geneviève was there, along with two young actors she brought with her. They told us that Geneviève's enthusiasm about Anaïs was contagious. This was amazing, simply because there seems to be so few French people who know anything at all about Anaïs Nin, and here was one of France's elite actors who'd brought along some of the *Diaries*, having marked several passages. She never knew Anaïs, she told me, but fell in love with her writing years ago.

Jean-Hugues Anglade at the gate
Photo © Sky Blue Press

Everyone was sitting around a large table in the parlor, talking, laughing, and even though most of us were strangers to each other, we all were united in our anticipation about what the afternoon had in store for us. Jacques, once again, consulted his watch and announced "*Mesdames et Messieurs, il faut partir.*" We piled into two cars and were on our way.

So far, everything had gone according to Jacques' rigorous schedule, and he was not about to tolerate any delays. His driving, normally conservative, was determined. When someone came his way on one of the one-lane streets, he won out, even to the point where a burly truck driver was forced to back up and let us through.

We parked on the extremely narrow rue de Montbuisson, as the second car arrived. We were greeted at the green pedestrian gate by Jean-Hugues Anglade, who took the time to shake each of our hands, graciously welcoming us to his new home. He led us into the courtyard where we were all agape for several moments.

Jean pointed out the old barn-like structure to the right of the courtyard where Hugo's car was kept in the thirties.

In the front there is a gravel driveway, and a pool which is now filled with dirt and planted with ivy. The fountain emerges like the headstone of a tomb (3).

When Jean found out that there had been a pool and fountain in the courtyard, he was incited to find out where they were, expressing a desire to do what Anaïs had done: unearth and restore them. Jean is sincere about his desire to restore the house according to some of Anaïs's descriptions. It seemed too good to be true until later on when we saw an old garden bench he'd found in the back of the house and fixed.[5] Now it sits proudly in front of the house, intact, a symbol, perhaps, of what is to come.

[The house] seemed to have sprouted out of the earth like a tree, so deeply grooved it was within the old garden. It had no cellar and the rooms rested right on the ground. Below the rug, I felt, was the earth. I could take root there, feel at one with the house and garden, take nourishment from them like the plants (4).

The house is carved into a hill, and the back, being on the taller side of it, seems lower to the ground than the front, as if buried. A huge tree dominates the garden—it may be as old as the house, if not older. Some of its limbs were cut off for firewood during World War II, giving it a tragic aura, like a limbless Greek statue. Its roots are deep, most likely penetrating the entire property. A swing set for Jean's children symbolizes his own efforts to "take root there."

When we finally stepped foot inside the house, I had the feeling of having come full circle. The haunting dreams were over, and my and many others' hopes and wishes for the house suddenly seemed fulfilled. To walk in this living house was to celebrate.

The room to the left of the entrance was the one that has intrigued me for years. In this room Anaïs had installed a turquoise mosaic fireplace, one of her finishing touches as she and Hugo first moved in, in 1930. In 1990, Noel Riley Fitch, one of Nin's biographers, sneaked into the house with her husband. She snapped several photographs[6] before being chased out by someone who was upstairs, and one photo was of this room. In it there hung from the beams a chandelier that resembled a gigantic, decaying flower. Underneath it was a dilapidated pool table. Fitch reported that the fireplace had been dismantled and was set aside. The room is now a music room in which Jean has guitars and amplifiers. Only a small brass lantern hangs from the beams today, and there is no trace of the fireplace.

The back of the house
Photo © Sky Blue Press

As Jean led us to the kitchen, he opened what looked like the door of a small pantry. Behind this door, however, lay the historical beginnings of the house. The walls of this small cavern were solid stone. On the floor was gravel. It was chilly, humid, and reeked of antiquity. "Looking in here," Jean said, "is like looking into the days before the revolution."

The kitchen is large with dramatically arched ceilings and small windows cut through at least two feet of stone, allowing the light to enter in shafts. At once we were reminded of the movie "Henry & June," the scene in which Hugo comes home early while Anaïs and Henry are upstairs engaged in passionate lovemaking. The maid leads Hugo into the kitchen, where she pours him coffee and sticks a freshly baked loaf of bread in his mouth, desperately trying to buy Anaïs some time. In the same movie, it is from this kitchen that Hugo and Anaïs emerge and are taken aback by Henry and his wife June's display of sexual hunger for each other in the next room. Anaïs doesn't write much about the kitchen in her *Diary*, and Joaquín Nin-Culmell, her brother, doesn't even remember it. It remains a mystery room.

We were then led to the parlor, which is on the second floor. We climbed the narrow, steep, circular staircase, walked to the south side of the house, and entered the large room, the centerpiece of which was a very old fireplace, one that was surely there when Anaïs was. The sunlight entering the windows transformed each of the guests into highly contrasted, timeless silhouettes. I looked at the entranceway and imagined Anaïs in a flowing gown pausing before entering the room.

The conversation, most of it in French, was lively and non-stop. Jacques recounted some of his *histoires de Louveciennes* for his new neighbor, drawing laughter and interest. Geneviève proposed a toast to Anaïs on her hundredth birthday, and we all raised our glasses.

From left: Jean-Hugues Anglade, Geneviève Casile, Anne-Marie Thomas
Photo © Sky Blue Press

Every room is painted a different color. As if there were one room for every separate mood: lacquer red for vehemence, pale turquoise for reveries, peach color for gentleness, green for repose, grey for work at the typewriter (5).

Jean's professional assistant, who has worked with him for fifteen years, took us on another tour, showing us a spot where the paint had been peeled off because the law requires searching for and removing lead-based paint whenever a house changes hands. The bottom layer was turquoise, Anaïs's color of reverie. I imagine each room in the house has her colors underneath. How fascinating it would be to uncover each of them and document them. The colors in the rooms nowadays are earthy: terra cottas, yellows, greens, oranges, and the view through the doorways in a straight line reminded me of a kaleidoscope.

In the bathroom on the second level was a well-worn antique bathtub, one that obviously has been there for many decades. The porcelain has been worn off on the outside under the edge of the tub from generations of bathers gripping it to get in and out. Surely, the bathers included Anaïs and Hugo, most likely Henry, Rank, cousin Eduardo, brother Joaquín...

There are eleven windows showing between the wooden trellis covered with ivy. One shutter in the middle was put there for symmetry only, but I often dream about this mysterious room which does not exist behind the closed shutter (4).

We climbed more stairs to the third floor. On both the second and third floors, there was no evidence of a sealed window. In each case, there were three windows on the outside, and three on the inside as well. However, on the second floor, there was one window that, although it allowed the light in, gave only on the hallway from behind large, curving beams. Perhaps at some point since Anaïs's departure,

the window was put in—it is conceivable that there was nothing behind it beforehand.

When I look at the large green iron gate from my window it takes on the air of a prison gate. An unjust feeling, since I know I can leave the place (4).

The gate as seen from inside
Photo © Sky Blue Press

Looking out the window onto the courtyard, the iron gate does loom formidably, as it does from the street. It is the same gate that first kept Anaïs inside, and ultimately locked her out. The same gate Hugo used when he took his car out. The same gate by which Anaïs's father entered. The same gate, restored, green as it always has been. We were in the house looking at it, realizing how incredible it was to be able to.

While the house was very symbolic for Anaïs, for those of us who were there that day, it was a manifestation of her dreams and visions. For each of those literary and psychological rooms, there exists its tangible counterpart, an extension of her inner being. To walk through the house was to walk through Anaïs's psyche. We all could have easily imagined ourselves as characters in *House of Incest*, traversing the house at the tip of Anaïs's pen.

As soon as I go to Paris too often, my mother looks disapprovingly out of her window, and does not wave good-bye... My brother Joaquín plays the piano continuously, as if he would melt the walls... (5).

On the third level there are several small rooms connected by a hallway. It was in these rooms Anaïs's mother and brother lived. Joaquín remembers playing his piano there, way up on that top floor, developing and refining his skills. The windows form the dormers atop the house, which give on the courtyard. Anaïs's conscience seems to be personified by her mother, whereas the courtyard represents a launch pad for escape into a world where she felt free and alive. Looking up at those small windows, I tried to imagine what the face would have looked like. Ghost-like, perhaps. Anaïs said it reminded her of the old women in the village who stared out of their windows whenever she and Hugo took their dog for a walk.

Across the courtyard is the house next door, tall, foreboding with its bricked up windows. There was no one threatening us, ordering us away. I am not certain who lives in that house today...it seemed silent and dead, as 2 bis once did.

When we returned to the parlor, many strands of conversation were going simultaneously. The gathering had been a rousing success, a true celebration of life. Guests were beginning preparations to leave—I was amazed at how quickly the afternoon had passed. All of us came together at the gate where farewells were exchanged and pictures were taken to commemorate the occasion.

In a way, I was anxiously looking forward to pondering what had happened, to digest it, to think and dream about it, just as much as I was happy to be there. I looked forward to writing about it, talking about it, examining the photos, sharing the experience in any way possible. Louveciennes lives. Louveciennes has a kind and caring owner who possesses an artist's sensibilities, a scientist's curiosity, and respect for the past. When we left, it was a triumphant departure.

There is much about the house that remains hidden behind the haze of mystery. Claudine said that the style of the house indicates that is was not built for the aristocracy, that it was built out of inexpensive materials, the beams are all exposed, and the layout of the many rooms suggests that perhaps it was built as lodging for workmen on a plantation or vineyard. Monique told us that she had done research on the house and found no official documentation earlier than 1803, which would make it seventy years newer than Anaïs reported it to be. *Mystère et boules de gomme*, as they say, mysteries hopefully to be solved in the near future.

In the meantime, Jacques has put down his baton, having successfully conducted a series of historic moments, and has taken his bows. Anne-Marie is planning an event based on Anaïs Nin in Louveciennes this autumn. Geneviève is continuing to spread the word. Jean-Hugues is continuing his restoration. Louveciennes lives. ◈

The bathtub
Photo © Sky Blue Press

Notes

---

[1] Sisyphus, sentenced to endlessly pushing a rock to the top of a mountain only to have it roll back down, is considered by Camus to be the epitome of the "absurd hero" in his retelling of the myth. Sisyphus is aware of the vain hope he will succeed, and therein lies the tragedy. According to Camus, however,

Sisyphus is also aware of the degree of his own misery. This recognition of his destiny transforms his suffering into his victory. It has to be a victory, for as Camus says:

> I leave Sisyphus at the foot of the mountain! One always finds one's burden again. But Sisyphus teaches the higher fidelity that negates the gods and raises rocks. He too concludes that all is well. This universe henceforth without a master seems to him neither sterile nor futile. Each atom of that stone, each mineral flake of that night-filled mountain, in itself forms a world. The struggle itself towards the heights is enough to fill a man's heart. One must imagine Sisyphus happy.

[2] See www.skybluepress.com for a detailed map.

[3] See www.ville-neuillysurseine.fr/html/decouv/histoire.asp for a timeline of Neuilly's history.

[4] See *Diary 7*, pg. 143. There is, in the same volume, a photograph of A.N. standing outside the gate.

[5] A photo of this bench and a twin can be found in *ANAIS: An International Journal*, vol. 11, 1993, pg. 5.

[6] Some of the photos can be found in *Anaïs Nin: A Book of Mirrors*, Sky Blue Press, 1996, pp. 21-24.

Louveciennes is dead. It was dismantled... When I arrived I found the auctioneers had moved everything out in the front yard, and were holding the auctions out of doors.

Beds, curtain, carpets, tables, desks, chairs, bookcases, pillows, bedspreads, all the intimate furnishings of a house so much loved and lived in, so saturated with memories. It seemed to me that when strangers opened the drawers, words would come out, that when they shook the curtains, one would hear the voice of Artaud, Allendy, Joaquín, Henry and June, my father, Jeanne, others.

...When it grew dark, and the sale was still going on, the empty house lit up by naked bulbs shone out once more like a mosque, with its gorgeous colors in contrast to the grey muted village, shone out once more, warm, sparkling, and then died (Diary 2, 138-139).

Book reviews and multimedia

The New Nin Criticism

A Review of Anaïs Nin's Narratives. *Edited by Anne T. Salvatore. University Press of Florida, 2001. 290 pages. ISBN 0-8130-2113-8.*

A study of the responses to Anaïs Nin might be just about as interesting as her work and life. She got it all: puzzled or hostile dismissal alongside adulation; angry objections to her style, ideas, and behavior right beside worshipful admiration for same; the support as well as the enmity of feminists; the approval of Freudians and their kin, who applauded her psychoanalytic perspectives, as well as aspersions from critics who accused her of committing therapeutic outpourings instead of creating literature. All these responses, and more, have tended to be both polarized and polarizing, inciting insults from opposing camps and hardening opinions rather than opening the way to nuanced analysis and criticism.

Now a new generation of academic readers, well represented in this collection of essays, is weighing in, and we should welcome them. The contributors to this book have at least two constructive and calming traits in common: they are taking Nin seriously and their point of departure is objective scholarship, not defensive or accusatory personal reaction. As Anne Salvatore, a professor at Rider University, puts it in her introduction, these writers believe Nin's narratives are worthy of "exacting scholarly study" (1). And that is precisely what we get. If these writers tilt in favor of Nin, most take great pains to be rational and expository in their favoritism.

We have, for example, a dense, detailed, and intelligent study of Nin's erotic stories published in *Delta of Venus* and *Little Birds*. Here, Diane Richard-Allerdyce explores how Nin manages to subvert the idea of sexual exploitation while seeming to write the kinds of stories that depend on this very trope.

We have several approaches to what the contributors have the grace to admit is often obscure fiction. Suzette Henke calls the five novellas of *Cities of the Interior* Nin's "Proustian magnum opus" (61) and recognizes that the reader needs a skilled guide to navigate the "improbable psychic journeys, surrealistic interior dreamscapes, and a fiercely focused avant-garde exercise in psychoanalytical characterization" (61). Henke takes on the responsibilities of steering us through one of the novellas, *A Spy in the House of Love*, and she is a helpful escort. A second essay by Diane Richard-Allerdyce takes on *House of Incest* from the point of view of Lacanian theory; this will be especially useful to those who understand Lacanian theory. And Sharon Spencer, focusing on the novelette "Winter of Artifice," describes how Nin sought to make music of her prose and to borrow structure from the symphony, imagery from paintings, and rhythms from dance.

Maxie Wells treats *Spy* along with *Seduction of the Minotaur* in a fascinating essay that differentiates Nin's work from both formal modernism and feminist modernism and credits her with, in effect, the creation of an original, even prototypical, version of what has since been called *écriture féminine*. Wells also proposes that Nin's version of what became the domain of French writers in the 1970s, notably Hélène Cixous, Luce Irigaray, and Julia Kristeva, was less body-centered and thus more complex. Nin was more expansive and inclusive than her French successors by expressing the "ways in which a female body reflects the female mind" (214).

Philippa Christmass contributes what may be the strongest—or at least the most lucid—essay in the collection with a study of Nin's fiction and its place in the emerging feminist/modernist canon. Christmass argues that women writers in general have not received their full due in the development of modernism *per se*, with all its rebellious nonconformity, and that Nin has been an invisible force within this heretofore invisible group—a shadow within a shadow. The essay urges us to realize that women writers were the "truly radical arbiters of modernism" (195) and that Nin worked at the very portals where both feminist inquiry and modernist study must begin (192). Christmass also points out that what was often taken for granted in the works of male modernists, i.e., the apolitical, the self-indulgent, and the impenetrable, was condemned in the work of women, especially Nin. While many a man received an invitation to the modernist club because of his "commitment to experimentation with narrative form and thematic content," Nin received "an invitation to invisibility" for exactly the same thing (200).

The vexed questions of how literally Nin's life fed her work and how accurately her work reflected her life comes up, as it must, in most of these essays as does her reliance upon the language and theory of psychotherapy. Anne Salvatore looks at all this in a discussion of Nin's uneasy experience with motherhood in several of its forms—her relationship with and portrayal of her own mother, her tendency to mother her lovers, her dramatic refusal to become a mother, and her fictional characters' struggle with all the above and other related dilemmas. Ellen G. Friedman looks at how Nin's relationship with her father, whether incestuous in fact or in imagination, provided a "constellation of ideas having to do with structures enforcing patriarchal values" (80). Thomas M. March deals with how Nin combines and conflates reality and imagination as well as internal and external signifiers, myth and actuality, and the roles of character and narrator. Just as Diane Richard-Allerdyce maintains that Nin's pornographic writing subverts the very traditions of titillation, March maintains that Nin subverts numerous other forms, including the traditional role of the narrator by employing his or her authority only to "nullify that authority" (169).

A not dissimilar argument appears in Marion N. Fay's article on the oft-repeated criticism that Nin lacked a social conscience. Her focus on the inner life, Fay insists, was not an escape from the outer world but her particular means of getting at and/or to it. Nin undermines the typically destructive methods of dealing with world affairs by insisting that a prerequisite to social solutions is the solution of personal problems. (If there is a theme running through these essays, it is Nin's gift for subversion of several kinds.)

Finally, Mai Al-Nakib closes out the book by suggesting that Nin's work cannot really be understood in terms of conventional forms of criticism but might be accessible via something called "rhizomatic" theory, named for that which "is constantly in motion, always in between things, and never identic" (254). Nin's work is forever evolving, on the move, contradicting itself, making itself up as it goes along, both fearless and fearful, secret and public, at once seeking roots and wings, limits and limitlessness, order and chaos—in sum indefinable, resistant to categories, and resisting classification. Thus we need an equally expansive and elastic critical language in order to deal with this eel-like œuvre. Maybe the language of the rhizome will do the trick.

Which brings me to the problem here. The academy, as represented by these scholars, *is* taking Nin seriously, providing the frameworks for objective analysis, and mercifully removing her from warring camps of lovers and haters. At the same time, this work tends to be itself obscure. The prose here is often very hard slogging. All these essays are careful, sober, and intelligent. The book is well edited, nicely ordered, and often quite helpful in interpreting some of Nin's more abstruse writing. But turn to any one of these essays and you'll find sentences like these, way more abstruse than anything Nin wrote: "The construction of an internal externality is an act of naturalization of the mythological signification of encountered objects." "The narrator's interpolations may subordinate characters' consciousnesses, and thereby their realities, to her own, but these interruptions are represented as interpretations, not as reports of immutable external truths." Taking these out of context makes them worse, I realize, and I have deliberately not cited the pages of these two of many examples. I do not wish to single out any of these writers for doing what their jobs require and reward, and even the most lucid contributors here occasionally and naturally fall back on the tangled language of their métiers.

Still, it seems to me a shame—and an irony—that the very people who are finally giving Anaïs Nin the consideration she deserves are also putting up new walls that keep the "common reader" at a helpless distance. Those who turn to Nin for pleasure or comfort or help in healing their own fragmented souls (and Nin at least said she wrote for all her fellow-wounded and fellow-seekers) will not be tempted to look here for clarification. At the moment when the academy is rescuing Nin from one kind of prison, it is putting her in another. ◈

—*Jane Eblen Keller*

The Biographical Allure

A Review of Seduction: A Portrait of Anaïs Nin, *Margot Duxler. EdgeWork Books, 2002. 240 pages. ISBN 1-931223-02-5.*

Every biography is a story of seduction, and as such proceeds as much from the seduced as from the seducer. Of course, most biographers seek to minimize if not totally obliterate the traces of their personal fascination with their subjects. In *Seduction: A Portrait of Anaïs Nin*, Margot Beth Duxler honestly addresses the consequences of her friendship with Nin, and her own motivations for succumbing to the allure of Nin's invented selves.

In fact, Duxler's personal friendship with Nin makes her uniquely qualified to write the kind of biography she has set out to provide here. She begins to forge a compelling integration of the academic and the experiential, as she examines how her own seduction by the myth of Anaïs Nin as a liberated woman has been tempered by a disillusion that emerged after Nin's death with the revelation of her multiple lives and lies. The result has not been resentment on Duxler's part but an increased desire to understand the woman by whose persona(e) she has, by her own admission, been guided and inspired. The seductive quality of Nin's inventions is replaced, in Duxler's experience, by the equally seductive promise of understanding why Nin felt the need to deceive.

Duxler looks primarily to Nin's *Diary* in order to uncover the motivations for Nin's creation of multiple, fully realized, and seemingly contradictory selves. The urge to understand others, to recognize and validate the importance of individual experience, is a defining feature of Nin's novels and other fiction. Duxler has demonstrated her sincere and strong desire to understand, as well as her competence in wielding the critical tools with which to articulate a unique appreciation of the *Diary* as a narrative of discovery, compensation, compulsion, and creativity.

Duxler's book is at times a biography, a critical assessment of Nin's *Diary*, a primer on the psychological functions of diary writing, as well as a personal memoir of her own relationship with the various myths of Anaïs Nin. On one hand, this structure mirrors the elusive nature of Nin's identity, indeed of any biographical subject, whose self-representations and contested and disparate receptions by others constantly force a biographer to reevaluate and amend the portrait in progress. Then again, this results in a highly fragmented text, one that identifies the importance of several approaches to understanding Nin's development while only gesturing toward the implications of their full integration.

Although the biographical sections of the book rely somewhat heavily on ground already well trod by Deirdre Bair and Noel Riley Fitch, Duxler is unflinching in her exploration of the dangers of self-delusion and the pain that this inflicts on others—pain whose potential, as Duxler notes, Nin used to justify the extent and perpetuation of her many deceptions. As a psychological practitioner, Duxler brings a great deal to her elucidation of the etiologies of these personal struggles, while as a theorist she clearly articulates the boundaries of the *Diary*'s transformative artistic and self-reinforcing purposes. Duxler is at her best when she uses the *Diary* itself to trace the emergence of the most dramatic conflicts between Nin's competing, or at least disparate, selves.

Duxler's review of literary and psychological models of diary writing is impressive in the range of potential applications to Nin's *Diary* that it suggests. She provides a somewhat detailed summary of Thomas Mallon's categories of the various functions diaries serve in the lives of their creators, as well as of D.W. Winnicott's theories on the emergence and development of the self. It is clear from Duxler's brief commentary here that there is much to say about the manner in which the *Diary* evinces a full range of writerly and psychological motivations over the course of its composition.

The biographer is in a unique position to observe and collect, if not to resolve, the competing effects of a human being's inevitable deployment of multiple selves. And Anaïs Nin seems to have given life to every self she felt the need to be, in an ongoing process of seduction that has only begun to come to light after her death and with the publication of the unexpurgated *Diary*. Duxler seeks to illuminate the origins of and ongoing motivations that informed the development of Nin's often-captivating and intriguingly contradictory selves. There is

clearly an opportunity for further consideration of how models like Mallon's and Winnicott's can inform a study of the initiation and evolution of both the compensatory and narrative functions of Nin's *Diary*—and why it continues to wield such seductive power. ◈
—*Thomas March*

An Argument for Further Study

A glance at the Nin-Miller chapter in Literary Liaisons: Auto/ biographical Appropriations in Modernist Women's Fiction, *by Lynette Felber, Northern Illinois University Press, 2002. 232 pages. ISBN 0-87580-301-6.*

sing a theoretical framework—feminist, Lacanian, Kristevan, and genre-based—Lynette Felber's new book, *Literary Liaisons*, examines what is termed "appropriation" from literary/romantic relationships by modernist women writers— in other words, claiming literary ownership of the relationship within their fiction. Felber uses a consistent and well thought out approach to examine relationships involving Anaïs Nin, Rebecca West, Zelda Fitzgerald, Radclyffe Hall, and H.D., revealing a common struggle for feminine identity and subjectivity.

In the cases examined in *Literary Liaisons*, Felber incorporates excerpts from the fiction inspired by literary/romantic partners into her template in order to explain the nature and outcome of the work as connected to the relationship. While theoretical and analytical language is utilized to a certain degree, clear and helpful explanations in the introduction render the reader free to roam the pages with few interruptions, which is an achievement for an academic book.

While all the cases are interesting and enlightening, of primary interest here is the study of the relationship between Anaïs Nin and Henry Miller in the chapter entitled "Anaïs Nin's Appropriations." Refreshingly, Felber views Nin as a "woman autobiographer who gestures toward a postmodern view of the self " rather than a mere "liar," as some of her biographers have charged, although she balances her statement by saying the accusation is partially due to Nin's refusal to "distinguish between her true autobiographical story and the fictional lives she creates." She prefers to look upon Nin's heavily edited *Diary 1* as autobiographical fiction, and the narrator as a textual persona.

Felber notes that early in the Nin-Miller relationship, there was a brief period of serene productivity and a certain degree of collaboration. Nin said during this period, "I have given him depth, and he has given me concreteness." Miller's "street language" quickly found its way into Nin's diary (*Henry and June* in particular) and in the published erotica. On the other hand, Nin's writing, while earning Miller's respect, incited him to parody, a form of writing that can "function as textual retribution" and "can be playful as well as belittling as well as destructive." *Scenario*, Miller's parody of discarded passages of Nin's *House of Incest*, drew her ire (she called it a "caricature" of her writing) and a sense of betrayal since *Scenario* was supposed to have been a collaborative work. Furthermore, according to Felber, another Miller parody, "Into the Night Life," seems to "not take seriously Nin's earnest effort to create a symbolic text through an interior suggesting the psychoanalytic process of communication with the unconscious." She is quick to add that "the *précieuse* style of her prose poem makes it vulnerable to parody," although, despite what appears to be belittlement, Miller did at least recognize her status as a writer. Nin's response to Miller's parodies did not come in the form of those of her own, but rather she "appropriated his literary subject, his wife, using the June portraits to develop a critique of the masculinist values under pinning his aesthetic practice."

June appears in several forms of Nin's writing, from the ethereal novels of the thirties and forties to *Diary 1*, released in 1966, and the more graphic *Henry and June*, published some twenty years later. There are several arguments concerning the "appropriation" of June into Nin's fiction. For example, Felber cites Hélène Cixous, who says that man wants to "keep woman in the place of mystery," whereas Nin wishes to understand. She mentions Kent Ekberg's theory that the Nin-Miller-June triangle is an "Oedipal triangle" re-enactment of the mother-father-daughter triangle Nin faced in her childhood, which seems to parallel the thoughts of other analysts and critics who believe that Nin has recreated a sort of mother-figure with her portrait of June, which in turn fits nicely with the Lacanian view of the "pre-mirror-stage" mother through whom the daughter finds her own identity. Felber uses several passages from the novels and the *Diary* to substantiate these interlocking theories. She carefully analyzes *House of Incest*, which characterizes Nin's birth from the womb of the "phallic mother"—June—and whose symbolism exemplifies clearly the mother-child fusion between them.

Important to Felber's study is the examination of the various *Diary* passages concerning the brothel at 32 rue Blondel in Paris, where Nin observes two female prostitutes engaged in lovemaking. Felber theorizes that in both the expurgated and unexpurgated versions Nin is experimenting with the notion of a "woman-to-woman bond," one that the patriarchal "Other" cannot truly understand and from which he is excluded. In the *Diary 1* passage, she appears to be exposing Miller to what he fails to grasp in his portrait of June, while in the *Henry and June* version, Nin takes ownership of the incident, fantasizing herself as June's lover while her husband Hugo looks on. Felber suggests that Nin has revised Freudian theory to the point at which "the penis is now extraneous," resulting in the "acquisition first of gender identity, then of libido." She adds that the rue Blondel passages, in which Nin does not exclude man or transcend patriarchy but emphasizes the female as subject (Miller or Nin's husband Hugo appear in each version as the "Other"), is an indication that she intended to be an "aesthetic mediator between the sexes." The conflict between the role of female-to-male mediator and the role of a feminine writer who emphasized the differences between the sexes is a contradiction that Felber believes ultimately damaged Nin's literary status.

Although Miller publicly defended and promoted Nin's diary as a major literary work, he was actually ambivalent about her habit of writing it because he felt it hindered her "creative" writing, her fiction. At one point, both he and Nin's psychotherapist, Otto Rank, tried to convince her to give up the diary altogether, unwittingly helping her to forge an artistic identity borne out of rebellion against her male mentors, not unlike other women of the same era who defined their literary selves by defying partriarchy. Part of the problem, according to Felber, is that her reactionary struggle to retain the diary was to choose "a subgenre often considered feminine and stigmatized accordingly." Furthermore, while Nin claimed that she wished to "write as a woman, and as a woman *only*," Felber believes she wrote *House of Incest* for Miller and Rank also, perhaps to prove her creative energy had *not* been depleted by the diary—another example of Nin's conflicting efforts to write "as a woman" while trying to "please men."

The conclusion that what gained Nin fame and success in the feminist-age sixties and seventies is also what ironically seems to keep her from entering the literary canon makes for a thought-provoking end to a chapter that seems to beg further study. Since Felber wishes "to contribute not only to a reevaluation of Nin but also to an emerging but still underdeveloped scholarly analysis of her text," perhaps this is precisely what she intended. ❖

—*Paul Herron*

"Spy in the House of Love" (1998 BBCfour.)

This documentary, which is actually a series of interviews with those in Nin's circle, takes on some of the sticky issues that have been presented by *Incest* and by Deirdre Bair's biography. Rupert Pole sits at a table in the Silver Lake house and expresses some bitterness he feels regarding Hugh Guiler's hold on Anaïs, refusing to "let her go"; Deirdre Bair moralizes that those following Nin's example often find themselves lonely and broken in the end; and Joaquín Nin-Culmell wrestles with the notion that his sister had an incestuous relationship with their father. Tristine Rainer offers comic relief as she attempts to read one of Nin's sex passages from the unexpurgated *Diary*. Peter Owen, Renate Druks, and John Ferrone are among the others interviewed.

"The Student of Prague" (1913 Paul Wegener, Fritz Wedmann. The New York Film Annex, 1618 West 4th St., Brooklyn, NY 11223.)

This is the film that provided the catalyst for Otto Rank's doppelganger theory, which influenced Nin. The main character of the film is introduced to his double after selling his soul to a mysterious man. The result is cataclysmic. www.nyfavideo.com.

"L'âge D'or" (1930 Luis Buñuel and Salvador Dalí. The New York Film Annex, 1618 West 4th St., Brooklyn, NY 11223.)

Banned for fifty-nine years, this monumental Surrealist film was accused of blasphemy and touched off riots in theatres in France. This is also the film for which Henry Miller wrote a rousing review, prompting Nin to revel in his explosive language and set the stage for their famous meeting. www.nyfavideo.com.

"Entr'acte" (1924 René Clair. Glenn Video Systems, 6924 Canby Ave., Ste. 103, Reseda, CA 91335.)

"Entr'acte" was to have been shown during the intermission of one of the early Surrealistic plays staged in Paris. The nudity of the actors, among other things, caused the play to be shut down, but this innovative and beautiful piece of moviemaking has survived. In the movie are many of the time's most prominent artists, such as Francis Picabia, Erik Satie, Man Ray, and Jean Cocteau, and several views of the Paris Nin and Miller knew.

"Henry and June" (1994 ISBN 1-898141-21-5. Castle Communications.)

Excerpts from the unexpurgated *Diary* by Cherie Lunghi. Lunghi's English accent is off-putting at first to those who are familiar with Anaïs Nin's speaking patterns, but once that has been pushed aside, Nin's writing carries the performance.

"Anaïs Nin Reads Excerpts from the *Diary of Anaïs Nin*" (1993 ISBN 1-55994-836-1. Caedmon/Harper Audio, 105 53rd St., New York, NY 10022.)

Excerpts read by Nin during lecture tours. Hearing Nin's voice reading her own work is worth the price of admission itself. Excerpts include her humorous "Ladders to Fire" anecdote, in which firemen refuse to believe Nin when she tells them of an apparent apartment fire because she has a French accent. Another is her classic debate with Henry Miller and Lawrence Durrell over "the woman's way" in writing at a Parisian café. www.harpercollins.com.

Internet

www.skybluepress.com. This site contains a link to the companion site of *A Café in Space*. There, one can find links concerning each of the articles for further study, a means to give feedback, share information, ask questions, do research, coordinate events. Its goal is to unite Nin study around the world.

www.anaisnin.com. The original Nin web site and the one that is most likely the most visited. Provided is a guest book, a news/events board, notes on scholarship, and links to various Nin books.

www.henrymiller.org. The official Miller Memorial Library web site. It has information about Miller's work, his friends and associates, other Miller links, and a schedule of events at the Big Sur facility.

www.lawrencedurrell.org. The Lawrence Durrell Society web page, which includes just about anything you would want to know about the English novelist whose artistic sensibilities attracted Nin during the Villa Seurat years in Paris.